ROUTLEDGE LIBRARY EDITIONS:
ENERGY ECONOMICS

Volume 25

ENERGY AND MATERIALS IN THREE SECTORS OF THE ECONOMY

ENERGY AND MATERIALS IN THREE SECTORS OF THE ECONOMY

A Dynamic Model with Technological Change as an Endogenous Variable

ALFRED LINDEN LEVINSON

Routledge
Taylor & Francis Group
LONDON AND NEW YORK

First published in 1979 by Garland Publishing, Inc.

This edition first published in 2018
by Routledge
2 Park Square, Milton Park, Abingdon, Oxon OX14 4RN

and by Routledge
605 Third Avenue, New York, NY 10017

Routledge is an imprint of the Taylor & Francis Group, an informa business

British Library Cataloguing in Publication Data
A catalogue record for this book is available from the British Library

ISBN: 978-1-138-10476-1 (Set)
ISBN: 978-1-315-14526-6 (Set) (ebk)
ISBN: 978-1-138-50269-7 (Volume 25) (hbk)
ISBN: 978-1-315-14507-5 (Volume 25) (ebk)

Publisher's Note
The publisher has gone to great lengths to ensure the quality of this reprint but points out that some imperfections in the original copies may be apparent.

Disclaimer
The publisher has made every effort to trace copyright holders and would welcome correspondence from those they have been unable to trace.

Energy and Materials in Three Sectors of the Economy:

A Dynamic Model with Technological Change as an Endogenous Variable

Alfred Linden Levinson

Garland Publishing, Inc.
New York & London, 1979

Library of Congress Cataloging in Publication Data

Levinson, Alfred Linden, 1933–
Energy and materials in three sectors of the economy.

(Outstanding dissertations on energy)
Originally presented as the author's thesis, University of California, Berkeley.
Bibliography: p.
1. Technological innovations—United States—Mathematical models. 2. Energy consumption—United States—Mathematical models. 3. Natural resources—United States—Mathematical models. 4. Steel industry and trade—United States—Mathematical models. 5. Aluminum industry and trade—United States—Mathematical models. 6. Container industry—United States—Mathematical models. I. Title. II. Series.
HC110.T4L48 1979 330.9'73'092 78-75010
ISBN 0-8240-3983-1

All volumes in this series are printed on acid-free, 250-year-life paper.

Printed in the United States of America.

Energy and Materials in Three Sectors of the Economy: A Dynamic Model with Technological Change as an Endogenous Variable

By

Alfred Linden Levinson

A.B. (University of Pennsylvania) 1955
M.A. (University of California, Davis) 1967

DISSERTATION

Submitted in partial satisfaction of the requirements for the degree of

DOCTOR OF PHILOSOPHY

in

Agricultural and Resource Economics

in the

GRADUATE DIVISION

of the

UNIVERSITY OF CALIFORNIA, BERKELEY

Approved: Richard B. Norgaard
C. Roger Glassey
John P. Holdren

Committee in Charge

Energy and Materials in Three Sectors of the Economy: A Dynamic Model with Technological Change as an Endogenous Variable

By

Alfred Linden Levinson

Abstract

One of the major difficulties encountered when modelling the demand for energy and resources is the lack of an adequate method for introducing technological change into the model. The few models that attempt to take technological change into account do so in an ad hoc manner. Our emphasis is to explain embodied technological change and its effect on the technical coefficients of input-output models. The recursive programming method is used to dynamically model embodied technological change in three industries, steel, aluminum, and can manufacturing. The method is composed of two phases, the static and the recursive or dynamic. The static or short run phase uses a linear program to optimize production by the various technologies. The dynamic phase consists of an econometric submodel where the level of investment in the technologies, the marginal cost of the technologies, the supply of some of the material inputs, and the demand for the output of the industries are determined. The model we employ simulates the period 1947-1967 for the three industries. Using this model forecasts of the rate of adoption of new technologies in the three industries are made for the period 1968-1972. This model could be incorporated into any model that has an input-output submodel thereby determining the effect of embodied technological change on the technical coefficients endogenously using economic factors.

ACKNOWLEDGMENTS

During the course of this project, I have had the benefit of assistance, criticism, and encouragement from a number of people. I would particularly like to thank Professor Charles R. Glassey whose advice regarding the approach was invaluable. Professors Richard Norgaard and John Holdren provided comments and criticisms which improved both the content and readability of the final copy. Dr. Garo Missiria provided me with some studies on the steel industry. I wish to thank Mr. Charles Walker of the Can Division, Kaiser Aluminum and Chemical Corporation for some can making equipment data and for his insights into the can manufacturing industry. The staff of the departmental computer facility assisted in the use of the computer to run the model.

Philip Ritz, Bureau of Economic Analysis, U.S. Department of Commerce made available the worksheets of the 1947 400 Sector Input-Output table. Everard M. Lifting, Engineering-Economics Associates, made available his copy of the 1958 Input-Output table. I wish to thank Philip Ritz, and Abert Walderhaugh, Bureau of Economic Analysis, and Everard M. Lofting for their explanations of the intricacies of the structure of input-output tables.

Table of Contents

Table of Contents (Continued)

Table of Contents (Continued)

List of Tables

List of Figures

Chapter I

Introduction

1.1 Objectives

In view of the recent decline of the quality of various domestic energy and natural resources and the uncertain nature of the availability of foreign supplies, it is becoming increasingly important to be able to forecast more reliably the demand for energy and resources in the United States. This task has been made more difficult by the rapid change in energy and resource prices and in technologies. These changes have made it more difficult to measure the impact of alternative policy decisions on the current use of resources.

Since many resources such as oil, coal, steel, and aluminum are used as intermediate inputs in the industrial sector, input-output analysis is often used, in part, to make such forecasts. One of the major obstacles encountered is that it is not known how the input-output coefficients change over time; nor is it known how the coefficients are affected by changes in the prices of both the inputs and the outputs or how technological change affects the coefficients.

It is the latter upon which this dissertation focuses. The impact of technological change upon the utilization of selected materials and energy resources in the steel, aluminum, and metal can industries is examined in this study. Using the results obtained from this study, the relevant coefficients are then estimated.

The factors governing the discovery and rate of adoption of a new technology are varied and complex. A new technology may be developed by the industry, by another industry, or by an individual inventor outside of industry. The basic oxygen furnace for steel making for example was developed by a small steel manufacturer in Austria. Whereas the draw and iron method of making beverage cans was developed by the beer industry.

Technological change can refer to the introduction of a new product, e.g. the electric light bulb, a new process, e.g. the basic oxygen furnace, or small improvements in existing production practices. The former results in the improvement of the quality of consumption. The latter two forms of technological change occurring in the production process are usually measured as changes in productivity. In Johansen's terminology, embodied technological progress is defined as a favorable shift in the ex-ante production function which leaves the efficiency of the already established production units unaffected [12 ; 145]. This type of technological change affects the short-run macro production function only by influencing the distribution of the new capacity. Improvements in production practices don't require new investment and thus will not affect existing facilities. This change will cause a shift in the short-run macro production function even though no new investment has taken place. This form of technological progress is defined as disembodied technological change. Mansfield refers to this as

a change in technique rather than a change in technology [6; 22].

It is possible to separate the embodied effect from the disembodied effect. Belinfante [13], has done this for the steam electric power generating industry. To do this, he had to use the vintage of each power plant and the amount of investment in plant equipment by plant for each year. This type of data is not available for most industries and in particular the industries we have chosen to study. Furthermore Belinfante doesn't try to explain technological change, rather he merely attempts to measure it.

In view of this we have decided not to attempt to explain disembodied technological change, but to concentrate on embodied progress.

Our major concern is to develop a model that would explain the rate of adoption of an innovation in an industry. Of great interest are those innovations that have a major impact on the industry, e.g. the introduction of nuclear power plants into the electric utility sector, or the basic oxygen furnace in the steel industry. Such changes have a significant effect on the materials and energy consumed by those industries. Smaller innovations of the sort that tend to characterize technological change in the automobile industry may have a significant impact over the long run in the case where there are many such small innovations. The data needed to explain such innovations are generally not available. In the instances where the innovation has a major impact on the industry, some technical data on the innovation is generally available, although the quality of that data will vary among industries.

Aluminum and steel were chosen because there is a significant interplay between the two. After World War II aluminum replaced steel as the skin for many aircraft. In the late fifties steel replaced aluminum. During the 1960's and early 1970's there was a shift to aluminum away from steel in both cans and automobile engines. However there is now a shift back to steel engine blocks and steel plate cans. The use of coal in steel making has also been changing with the introduction of the basic oxygen furnace and the electric furnace.

There has been some controversy as to the effect of changes in factor prices on the direction of technological change. The dominant view in economics has been that firms wish to save the total cost for a given output. At the competitive equilibrium each factor is being paid its marginal value product. Thus all factors are equally expensive to firms and there is no incentive for firms to search for techniques to save a particular factor.

Ruttan [11], on the other hand, argues that factor prices will influence the type of technological change that takes place. Furthermore as prices change, firms are not limited to simply allocating resources among known technical alternatives. Instead they can allocate resources toward the development of new technologies which expand the opportunity to substitute less expensive factors for more expensive factors.

The situation in the industries we have chosen to study varies from industry to industry. The basic oxygen furnace (B.O.F.) is being adopted because of lower production and capital costs, a faster production rate, and higher product quality [8; 71]. Thus it would appear that the adoption of the B.O.F. is due more to a desire to reduce total costs and less to the relative difference between the prices of the factors.

Technological change in the aluminum industry, on the other hand, seems to support the relative price hypothesis. Since the cost of electricity may run as high as two-thirds of the total cost, aluminum companies have expended much effort to minimize the cost of the energy input. Historically this was accomplished by locating in areas of the country where electricity was cheap and by maintaining a research program to develop new technolgies that would require less electricity. Here the desire to reduce the use of a relatively expensive factor has determined the direction of technological change.

In the can manufacturing industry the goal has been to reduce the amount of tin used in tinplate, find substitute materials for tinplate, and improve the can manufacturing process [14]. The major developments in the can manufacturing industry have come from outside the industry. The impact extrusion technology was developed by the aluminum industry. The adaptation of the Drawn and Iron Technology to cans was made by a beer company. The reduction of tin in the tinplate and the development of thinner tinplate and tinless plate came from the steel industry. While the can manufacturing industry had long desired to be less dependent on insecure supplies of tin, most of the reduction in the use of tin in tinplate after World War II came about as a result of the competition between the aluminum and steel industries. Here the impetus for technological change came about as a result of non-economic factors or of economic factors outside the industry.

1.2 Updating

Since it usually takes 7-10 years to prepare an input-output table, it has become necessary to develop procedures, albeit mechanical, to update the tables to the current year in order to use them in any meaningful way. Several updating methods have been developed. The two most widely used are the RAS method and the Linear Programming method.

The RAS method is due to Stone and Brown and is based on two assumptions. The first is that the elements of each row of the input-output matrix between the year t and the year $t + v$ are affected by the same multiplicative factor r_{i+v} which can be thought of as the "degree of absorption" or "degree of substitution" measured by the extend to which commodity i has been substituted for other commodities as an intermediate input into industrial process. The second is that the elements of each column of the input-output matrix are simultaneously affected by a column factor, s_{j+v}, which can be thought of as the "degree of fabrication" measured by the extent to which commodity j has come to absorb a greater or smaller ratio of intermediate to primary inputs in its fabrication. Other than these factors the technical coefficients are assumed to be constant. If A^t is the input-output matrix for the year t then $\hat{r}^{t+q}A^t\hat{s}^{t+q}$ would represent an approximation of the input-output matrix for the year $t+q$, A^{t+q}, where $\hat{r}^{t+q}$, $\hat{s}^{t+q}$ are diagonal matrices of correction factors. The name of the method "RAS" is obtained from the formulation of the approximation $\hat{r}A\hat{s}$ for the updated matrix.

Let $Z^t = (Z^t_{ij})$ be the transaction matrix for the year t and $z^t = Z^t\iota$ is the intermediate demand vector for the year t where ι is the unit column vector.

Let $(\eta^t)' = \iota' Z^t$ is the intermediate input vector.

Let x^t be the total output vector for the year t and $\hat{x}^t$ be the diagonal matrix with elements x^t on the diagonal. In order to find $\hat{r}^{t+v}$, $\hat{s}^{t+v}$, we consider the following for the update year $t+v$

(1) $\hat{r}^{t+q}A^t\hat{s}^{t+q}$

(2) $A^{t+q}\hat{x}^{t+q}\iota = Z^{t+v}\iota = z^{t+v}$

(3) $\iota' A^{t+v}\hat{x}^{t+v} = \iota' Z^{t+v} = (\eta^{t+v})'$

substituting (1) for A^{t+v} we have

(4) $\hat{r}^{t+v}A^t\hat{S}^{t+v}\hat{x}^{t+v}\iota = z^{t+v}$

(5) $\iota'\hat{r}^{t+v}A^t\hat{s}^{t+v}\hat{x}^{t+v} = (\eta^{t+v})'$

But (4) and (5) is a non-linear system of equations in $\hat{r}^{t+v}$ and $\hat{s}^{t+v}$. They are also not independent since $\iota' Z^{t+v} = \iota'\eta^{t+v}$. Thus $\hat{r}^{t+v}$ and $\hat{s}^{t+v}$ can only be determined up to a multiplicative scalar. If $\hat{r}$ and $\hat{s}$ satisfy (4) and (5), then do so $\lambda\hat{r}$ and $(1/\lambda)\hat{s}$. In order to obtain a solution, an iterative procedure is used. First we set $\hat{s}^{t+v}$ equal to the unit matrix and solve (4) for $\hat{r}$ such that $_{(1)}\hat{r}^{t+v} A_t \hat{x}^{t+v} \iota = z^{t+q}$ where $_{(1)}\hat{r}^{t+v}$ is the solution for $\hat{r}^{t+v}$ of the first iteration. Then we replace $\hat{r}^{t+v}$ with $_{(1)}\hat{r}^{t+v}$ in (5) and solve for $\hat{s}$ such that $\iota' \, _{(1)}\hat{r}^{t+v} A^t \hat{x}^{t+v} \, _{(1)}\hat{s}^{t+v} = (\eta^{t+v})'$. Then we iterate a second time substituting $_{(1)}\hat{s}^{t+v}$ in (4) and solving for $\hat{r}$. The solution $_{(2)}\hat{r}^{t+v}$ is substituted in (5) and $_{(2)}\hat{s}^{t+v}$ is determined We continue iterating in this manner until we have found solutions for $\hat{r}^{t+v}$ and $\hat{s}^{t+v}$ satisfying both (4) and (5) simultaneously within the required degree of accuracy. Let

$$(\eta_j^t) = \eta^t, \quad \text{then} \quad \sum_j (\eta_j - \sum_i x_{ij}) = \sum_i (Z_i - \sum_j x_{ij})$$

is a necessary condition for convergence. Also the matrix A must be non-degenerate and have non-negative elements. The sum of the signed row changes must equal the sum of the column changes. In practice this condition will usually be met without being explicitly specified since

$$\sum_i (Z_i^{t+v} - \sum_j a_{ij}^t x_j^{t+v}) = \sum_j (\eta_j^{t+v} - \sum_i a_{ij}^t x_j^{t+v}) = \sum_i \sum_j a_{ij}^{t+v} - \sum_i \sum_j a_{ij}^t x_j^t$$

Thus if given a reasonable base year input-output matrix and a later year intermediate and total outputs, the RAS method produces a unique estimate of A^{t+v}.

Another prominent method of updating the technical coefficients is linear programming. While linear programming had been used in the 1950's to alter the coefficients for specific problems it appears the first attempt to apply linear programming was in 1962 by Matuszewski, Pitts, and Sawyer. While the RAS method attempts to update the coefficients by balancing the rows and columns successively, the linear programming approach seeks to update the coefficients by balancing the rows and coefficients simultaneously, the individual coefficients undergoing as little relative change as possible. The linear program is stated as follows:

Find a set of values $a_{ij}^{t+v} (i,j = 1,2, \ldots\ldots, n)$ such that

$$\sum_i \sum_j \left[(a_{ij}^{t+v} / a_{ij}^{t}) - 1 \right]$$

is a minimum subject to the constraints

$$\sum_i a_{ij}^{t+v} x_j^{t+v} = \eta_j^{t+v} , \quad j = 1, \ldots, n ,$$

$$\sum_j a_{ij}^{t+v} x_j^{t+v} = z_i^{t+v} , \quad i = 1 , \ldots, n$$

$$\frac{1}{2} \leq a_{ij}^{t+v} / a_{ij}^{t} \leq 2 \qquad i,j = 1, \ldots\ldots, n \tag{7}$$

The constraint (7) is included to prevent a_{ij}^{t+v} from increasing by more than 100% or decreasing more than 50%. Schneider [2] evaluated both methods using 1947 and 1958 80 sector input-output tables which were aggregated into 24 sectors. He compared this with the naive method i.e. just using the 1947 input-output matrix and assuming the coefficients remained constant between 1947 and 1958. He performed the comparisons for both the individual coefficients and the transaction matrix flows. He then updated the 1947 input-output matrix to 1958 by the three methods. The RAS method, in the large majority of cases offered the best predictions of the 1958 flows and coefficients. A cell-by-cell examination of the 1958 transaction table and the three estimated transaction matrices showed that the naive method gave the best prediction in 206 cells, the L.P. method in 201 cells, and the RAS method in 362 cells (these figures include ties). The L.P. method altered 24 of the 98 cells in the wrong direction. The RAS method altered 153 of the 563 cells in the wrong direction. The RAS method yielded the most small differences and the fewest large differences.

More recently Davis, Lofting and Sathay [3] performed a comparison of the L.P. and RAS methods. They used the 80 sector input-output tables for 1963 and 1967 aggregated to 50 sectors. Then they updated the 1963 input-output table to 1967. They also found that the RAS method predicted the coefficients better than the L.P. method. The results showed that the RAS method produced closer predictions in 1,295 cells and the L.P. method in 664 cells.

1.3 Forecasting: Using Input-Output Analysis

Perhaps the most extensive studies of forecasts using fixed coefficient input-output tables have been done by Tilanus [1]. He starts with 27 sector input-output tables for each year between 1948 and 1958. Using the 1948 input-output table he computes the intermediate demand for each succeeding year up to 1958. This process is repeated using successive input-output tables between 1948 and 1957. He then calculates the error between the computed intermediate demand derived from one of the previous years input-output tables and the actual intermediate demand. The square root of the median of the mean square errors for the succeeding year for the 27 sectors was 8.7%. The square root of the maximum mean square error for any sector was 13.4%. The square root of the median of the mean square errors for the third future year was 10.6%. But the maximum for any sector was 24.5%. While the errors for a forecast one year in the future was not bad, by the fourth year the maximum error was already quite large. The square root of the median of the mean square errors for the eighth future year was 14.4%. The square root of the maximum mean square error for any sector for the eighth future year was 48.2%.

Tilanus then tried another experiment. He took the input-output table for 1948 and used the RAS method to up date it to 1951. Then he took the total output for 1957 and computed a prediction of interemediate demand. The square root of the median of the square errors between the predicted and actual demand was 16% and the square root of the upper quartile of errors was 23%. This is quite high. He then updated the 1948 input-output table to 1954 and took the total output for 1957 and computed the intermediate demand for 1957. He obtained a square root of the median square error between the predicted and actual demand of 9.9% and a square root of the upper quartile of 15.6%. This is certainly much improved over the straight projections and may be adequate for short term perdictions. During this period (1948-1957) the economy of the Netherlands was continually expanding which might account for the relatively good prediction using the RAS method. Barker [10] conducted a similar experiment using 1954 and 1960 input-output tables for the United Kingdom and obtained similar results.

Both Tilanus and Barker experimented with time trends in the coefficients. Using ten input-output tables, Tilanus found that linear trends gave poorer results than using the coefficients of the most recent table. Barker produced a linear extrapolation of the coefficients of the 1954 and 1960 input-output tables, then from the 1963 total output projected the intermediate demand for 1963. His results were similar to those of Tilanus.

Recently attempts have been made to treat the coefficients as functions of economic factors. Hudson and Jorgensen [9] have attempted to incorporate the effect on the coefficients of price variations and technological change induced by price variations. Actually they only take into account the Hicks-neutral technological change. Their model is highly aggregated and they assume the price of an input is the same for all sectors. The variation in the coefficients are determined in the following manner:

The relative share of the jth intermediate input is determined from the identity

$$\frac{\partial \ln P_I}{\partial \ln P_j} = \frac{P_j * X_{jI}}{P_I * X_I} = \frac{P_j}{P_I} * A_{jI}$$

where P_I = price of the ith industry

X_I = output of the ith industry

X_{jI} = interemediate demand for the output of industry j

A_{jI} = the technological coefficient representing the input of the output of industry j per unit output of industry i.

Then by dividing the relative shares by the ratio of the price of the output of the jth industry to the price for the ith industry they obtain the coefficients

$$\frac{X_{jI}}{X_I} = A_{jI}$$

where A_{jI} is a function of the prices of the outputs of the other industries, price of capital, price of labor, and price of competitive inputs for the industry. The prices of the output of the ith industry are determined from the price possibility frontier which is represented by a function that is quadratic in the logarithms of the prices of the inputs into that sector. The resulting price possibility frontier provides a local second order approximation to any price possibility frontier.

$$\ln A_I + \ln P_I = \alpha_0^I + \alpha_k^I \ln P_k + \alpha_1^I P_1 + \alpha_m^I \ln P_m + \ldots.$$
$$+ \frac{1}{2}\left[\beta_{kk}^I (\ln P_k)^2 + \beta_{k1}^I \ln P_k \ln P_1 + \ldots..\right]$$

$$\frac{P_j * X_{jI}}{P_I * X_I} = \alpha_2^I + \beta_{jk}^I \ln P_k + \beta_{j1}^I \ln P_1 + \beta_{jj}^I \ln P_j + \beta_{jm}^I \ln P_m + \ldots$$

for all m sectors $m \neq j,k,l$, P_k is the price of capital, and P_l is the price of labor.

The price possibility frontier is defined as the frontier of the set of price possibilities. By duality in the theory of production one can characterize the production possibility frontier in terms of the price possibility frontier. The price possibility frontier is represented in the form $\pi(P_1,P_2, \ldots, P_n,A) = 0$ where π is the level of profit associated with the set of prices (p_i) and A is the index of technology. The price possibility frontier is homogenous; thus $\pi(\lambda P_1, \lambda P_2, \ldots, \lambda P_n) = \pi(P_1,P_2, \ldots, P_n) = 0$. Under constant returns to scale if the production possibility frontier is commodity-wise additive, then the price possibility frontier is commodity-wise additive and is represented in the form

$$\pi(P_1,P_2, \ldots P_n) = \pi^1(P_1) + \pi^2(P_2) + \ldots . \pi^n(P_n) = 0$$

where the functions (π^i) are strictly monotone and depend only on a single variable. The functions (π^i) are either homogeneous of the same degree or are logarithmic. If we represent $\pi(P_1,P_2, \ldots, P_n,A) = 0$ in the form $A \cdot P_1 = g(P_2,P_3, \ldots, P_n)$ or in logarithmic form we have $\ln A + \ln P_1 = \ln g(P_2,P_3, \ldots, P_n)$ where P_1 is the price of the output.

In this manner Hudson and Jorgensen constructed their own coefficients as a function of prices. Then using this matrix of input-output coefficients, which are a function of prices, linked to other sub-models (production, consumption, etc.) they obtain an inter-industry econometric model which they used to forecast energy consumption.

1.4 Intertemporal Change of the Coefficients

As we have demonstrated above, the changes in the coefficients over time can be significant. While there are many factors that can cause the coefficients to change over time, three have been identified as dominant causes; (1) technological change, (2) changes in the relative prices of substitutable inputs, and (3) changes in product mix of a sector.

In neoclassical economic theory technological change is defined as a change in the production function. This contrasts with substitution, as a choice within the context of a given production function. However Mansfield [6] argues that not all changes in the production function are due to technological change. Mansfield further distinguishes between technological change and changes in techniques. "A technique is a utilized method of production. Thus, whereas a technological change is an advance in knowledge, a change in technique is an alteration of the character of the equipment, production and organization which are actually being used" [6; 22].

In their attempts to study the change in the coefficients, Leontief, Carter, and Vacarra reject these distinctions, since in practice it is often impossible to distinguish between substitution and technological change. They simply refer to changes in the inputs to a sector as structural change. "In actual practice it is often difficult to draw the line between bonafide changes in technological possibilities and shifts among 'known' alternatives. What is known in the laboratory may not be known on the production line; a process that has been tried on a small scale in one country may have a long way to go before it is economic on a large scale in another country. There is a broad spectrum of possible interpretations to the term 'known techniques' .... the distinction is not very important. When a material or a component becomes relatively cheap, ways are found to use it more. Whether this involves reaching into an old file of instructions or making up new ones may not be an essential question" [7; 10].

However Vacarra [5; 82] notes that in countries like the United States it is not unreasonable to assume that changes in the technical relationships for an entire industry occur slowly and orderly. New products are introduced; new materials substituted for old; new technologies enter; and changes in relative prices induce the long run substitution of one basic material for another. But these changes won't affect the total capacity of an industry all at once. Existing capacity will continue to be used, while only new capacity will utilize the newer processes. Eventhough the basic oxygen furnace was perfected in 1954, as of 1972, 18 years later, only 53% of U.S. steel making capacity utilized this new process.

Mansfield further distinguishes between technological change and innovation. Where "innovation" is defined as "an invention applied for the first time", Mansfield concedes that this distinction is not always clear particularly when the inventor and innovator are the same firm. In this situation the final stages of development may involve a limited market test of the invention.

No matter how much one may disaggregate, the sector will still contain a certain amount of aggregation, e.g. if one has a sector containing only automobiles, one still has a certain amount of aggregation, large cars, small cars, four door cars, two door cars, cars with 4, 6 or 8 cylinder engines, etc. In terms of the inputs to the automobile sector, the automobile firms themselves might be unable to separate the inputs between different types of automobiles. It is for this reason that coke cannot be disaggregated from the products of Iron and Steel Blast Furnaces (SIC 331). Thus a change in the mix of goods produced by a sector might well change the technical coefficient. A shift in automobile production from 200 cu.in. 6 cylinder autos to 450 cu.in. 8 cylinder autos increases the quantity of steel required per car. Thus the technical coefficient representing the amount of steel required per dollar of automobile would most likely change.

While these appear to be the dominant causes of intertemporal change in the coefficients, there are many other causes of these changes. Shifts in classification might be a cause. Initially, missiles appeared in ordinance, then later were shifted to aircraft. A new item is usually part of an existing category until it becomes large enough to warrant its own category. Changes in quality of the good might also affect the coefficient. The recent requirement that all autos be equipped with smog devices that reduce the emission of nitrogen compounds, substantially increased the quantity of platinum required to produce an automobile. There are methods for avoiding the problem of quality changes altogether. Leontief avoids this problem by calling each year's output of any given industry a different product. This works in a dynamic context where he describes successive input structures with each year's outputs being produced from inputs produced in preceding years without requiring that the inputs or outputs be identical or comparable over time. This approach is not helpful if one is interested in studying how the coefficients change and does not give any clues as to future changes in the coefficients.

Another factor, which could cause intertemporal change in the coefficients, is the divergence of actual technical relationships from a linear homogeneous function and the strict proportional relationships between the changes which it assumes. The coefficients for a given year might differ from those of another year merely because the degree of capacity utilization was much greater in one year than the other.

Secondary production and competitive imports are handled as a transfer from either the secondary producer or importer to the primary producer of that product. This approach includes secondary production as both a part of the industry which produces it and also as part of the output of the industry to which it is primary. The secondary production is treated as if it is sold to the primary industry where it becomes part of the output available for distribution. Thus these transfers can cause spurious changes in the coefficients. Vacarra has adopted the procedure of excluding secondary flows and further computes the coefficients on a domestic rather than on a total output base.

The shift of purchases of an input from one industry to another industry could also cause changes in the coefficients. Steel for refrigerator doors might be purchased directly from the iron and steel sector one year and from the stamping sector in another year. Lastly some of the changes are no doubt due to random factors such as differences between the various input-output tables in the data sources, statistical methods for estimating the technical relationships, and the method for distributing the unallocated inputs.

Many, including Leonfief and Carter, have used temporal changes in the coefficients to study structural change in the economy. Few have attempted to study the factors causing the coefficients to change. Foressell [4] attempts to study the change in the coefficients for the 21 industries comprising the manufacturing of wood and cork, furniture and fixtures, and paper and paper products in Finland for the years 1954-1965. The 21 industries were chosen at the four digit SIC level. These industries form a recursive chain of outputs and principal raw material inputs. The factors he takes as causing change in the coefficients are technical development, relative prices of inputs, product mix, and change in the level of output.

As proxies for technical development, he used measures of the degree of electrification and mechanization, and time. He also assumed the functional relationship between the input-output coefficient and the factors causing it to change were linear. Due to the more highly industrialized nature of the United States' economy,

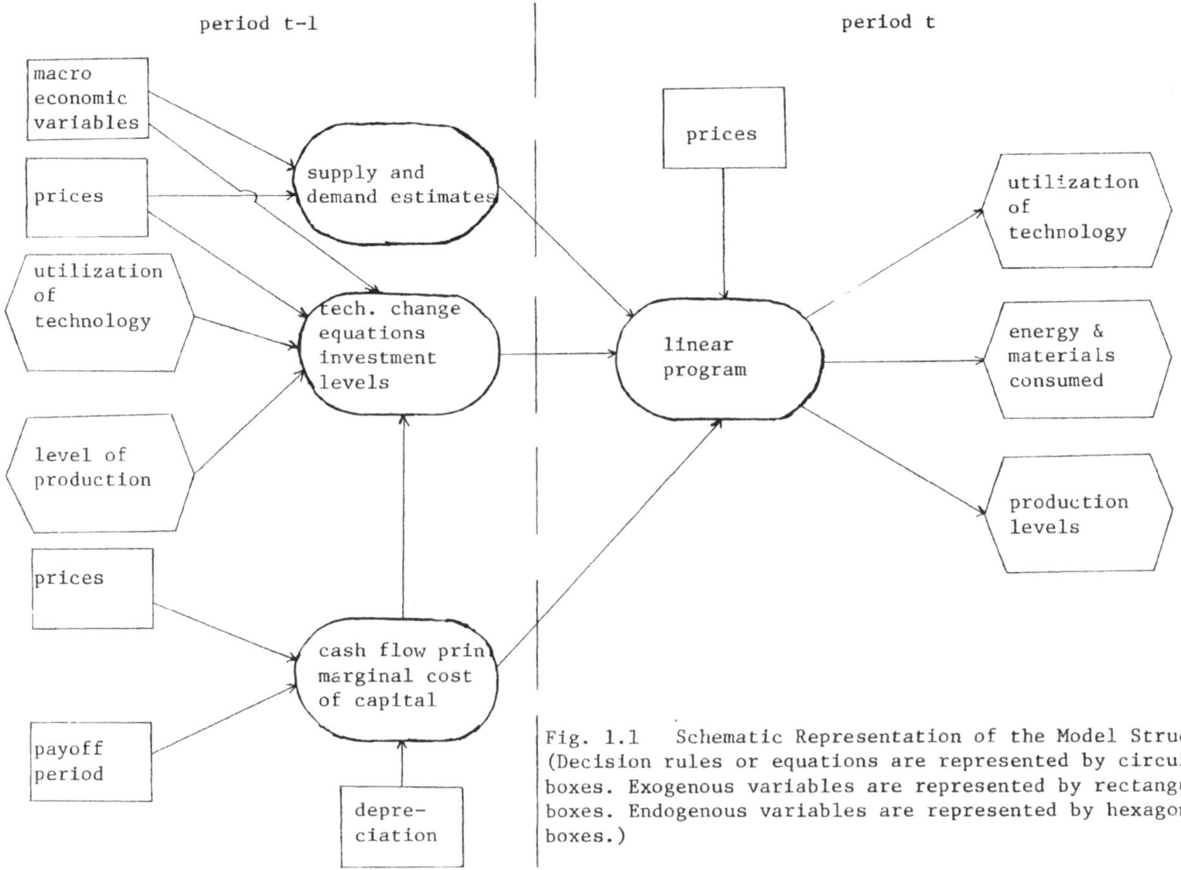

Fig. 1.1 Schematic Representation of the Model Structure (Decision rules or equations are represented by circular boxes. Exogenous variables are represented by rectangular boxes. Endogenous variables are represented by hexagonal boxes.)

this approach would not be appropriate.

The only other person mentioned in the literature as having studied this problem is Vaccara who apparently has not published any quantitative results.

1.5 Study Plan

The model that will be used in this dissertation as a basis for studying embodied technological change is the recursive programming model developed by Day [4]. It is a dynamic mixed linear programming econometric model. It is composed of two phases, the static and the recursive or dynamic. The static or short-run phase uses a linear program to optimize production during the period when no technological change occurs. It is this part of the model that produces the material and energy requirements. During the dynamic phase the level of investment in the various technologies, supply of and demand for the material, and energy inputs are estimated. A schematic representation of the model is given in Fig. 1.1. In period $t-1$ the level of investment in the various technologies, the cost of capital, and the supply and demand constraints are estimated from macroeconomic variables, the relative costs of using the technologies, and the prices of the inputs. In period t production is optimized using the linear program which determines the input requirements and the level of utilization of the technologies. The bounds on the linear program are estimated by the dynamic phase during period $t-1$. The above process is then repeated for successive time periods.

The model is used to simulate the period 1947-1967 and to forecast the period 1968-1972. The equations used in the dynamic phase are estimated for the period 1947-1967. These equations are then used to forecast the level of investment in the technologies, the supply, and demand for the period 1968-1972.

The steel, aluminum, and metal can industries were chosen as the focus of this study in order to examine the effect of the competition for the metal can market by the aluminum and steel industries on all three industries. As a prerequisite to modeling technological change, it is necessary to understand the development of those technologies under consideration. This is covered in the following three chapters.

In Chapter II the steel industry is discussed. The steel production process is described along with the historical development of the steel making technologies which are the technologies in the steel industry that are modeled. Factors governing the rate of diffusion of the basic oxygen furnace technology are also explored.

Chapter III contains an examination of the aluminum industry. The history of the development of the aluminum reduction technology is described. Since the production of aluminum is of recent origin, the industry has had to develop markets for the metal, often competing with other materials in current use in those markets. This orientation of the aluminum industry played a key role in the development of the two-piece beverage can. The development of markets for aluminum products is also covered in this chapter.

The can manufacturing industry is described in Chapter IV. The can making process is discussed along with the development of the can making technologies. Since the metal can industry faces competition on several fronts, the structure of the industry is examined. The threat of self-manufacture of cans by the canners and competition from bottles are investigated. Also included is a discussion of the interplay between aluminum and steel as materials for cans and its impact on technological change in the metal can industry.

In Chapter V the recursive programming model is developed. Day's recursive programming model is compared with the one used in this study. The differences in the treatment of investment in the technologies are analyzed.

The model is applied to the aluminum, steel, and metal can industries and the results are evaluated in Chapter VI. The behavioral equations of the dynamic phase are estimated for each of the industries. The level of investment in the various technologies, as predicted by the model, is compared with actual investment. Similarly the predicted capacity utilization, materials, and energy consumption are compared with the actual data.

The conclusions and extensions of the study are presented in Chapter VII. The study is evaluated; the problems encountered are discussed; and suggestions for improving and extending the study are presented.

References

1. Tilanus, C.B., Input-Output Experiments, The Netherlands 1948-1961, Rotterdam University Press, Rotterdam, 1966.
2. Schneider, Howard, An Evaluation of Two Alternative Methods for Updating Input-Output Tables, B.A. Thesis, Harvard University, 1965.
3. Davis, Lofting, and Sathaye, The RAS and LP Methods of Updating Input-Output Coefficients: A Comparison, unpublished, 1975.
4. Forsell, O., "Explaining Changes in Input-Output Coefficients for Finland", Brody and Carter, Input-Output Techniques, North Holland Publishing Co., Amsterdam, 1972.
5. Vaccara, Beatrice, "Changes Over Time in Input-Output Coefficients for the United States, Carter and Brody, Applications of Input-Output Analysis, North Holland Publishing Co., Amsterdam, 1970.
6. Mansfield, Edwin, Industrial Research and Technological Innovation, An Econometric Analysis, Norton & Co., Inc., New York, 1968.
7. Carter, Anne P., Structural Change in the American Economy, Harvard University Press, Cambridge, 1970.
8. U.S. Dept. of Labor, Technological Trends in Major American Industries, Bulletin No. 1474, 1966.
9. Hudson, E., and Jorgensen, D., "U.S. Energy Policy and Economic Growth, 1975-2000", The Bell Journal of Economics and Management Sciences, Autumn, 1974.

10. Barker, T.S., "Some Experiments in Projecting Intermediate Demand", Allen and Gossling, Estimating and Projecting Input-Output Coefficients, Input-Output Publishing Co., London, 1975.

11. Hayami, Yujiro and Ruttan, Vernon, "Factor Prices and Technical Change in Agricultural Development: The United States and Japan, 1880-1960, Journal of Political Economy, Sept.-Oct., 1970 78 (5), pp. 1115-41.

12. Johansen, L., Production Functions, North-Holland, Amsterdam, 1972.

13. Belinfante, A.E.E., Technological Change in the Steam Electric Power Generating Industry, Ph.D. dissertation, University of California, Berkeley, 1969.

14. Brighton, Pilcher, and Lueck, "Metal Cans of the Future", Food Technology, Sept., 1954, pp. 424-430.

Chapter II

The Steel Industry

2.1 Introduction

In order to understand technological change in the steel industry, it is necessary to study the steel making process and the development of the steelmaking technologies. Sometimes it is argued that the U.S. steel industry is laggard in adopting new technologies particularly when compared with Japan. Thus the rate of adoption new technologies by the U.S. and Japanese steel industries is investigated in this chapter.

2.2 Iron and Steel Technologies

In our model we have focused on the steelmaking technologies. The process of producing finished steel from iron ore involves much more than just the steelmaking technology. Both the metallurgical coal and the iron ore undergo transformation before entering the production process. The coal is converted to coke. Coking is a destructive distillation process in which coal is subjected to high temperatures in order to reduce its volatile content. The residue, which is the coke, contains 85-90 per cent carbon with the remainder in ash, sulfur, phosphorous, and other substances. Coke is used primarily as a fuel and source of carbon in the blast furnace production of pig iron. There are several processes for the production of coke. They are the beehive oven process, byproduct process, continuous process, and formcoke process. The most commonly used method is the byproduct process because many types of low quality coal can be utilized by blending with other coals, and the gas coal chemicals released can be fully recovered. Higher yields and more uniform coke are also obtained. Currently 98 per cent of all coke production is produced in byproduct ovens.

High capital costs associated with the construction of new iron and coke making facilities have induced the development of techniques to increase the capacity of the former and reduce the required coke input. One approach has been the use of iron ores of higher ferrous content and better physical structure. This has resulted in an increase in the use of imported high content ferrous ores and beneficiated ores.

Beneficiation is a broad general term that includes any method to improve the physical and chemical properties of the ore. Such methods include crushing, screening, blending, washing, grinding, concentrating, and agglomerating. Agglomeration is a technique whereby pieces of ore below a certain size, which cannot be used efficiently in a blast furnace, are bounded into uniformly sized lumps.

The next step in the steel making process is to convert the iron bearing raw materials into pig iron. Iron ores are largely iron oxides which must be reduced to iron. This task is accomplished in the blast furnace where the iron ore is mixed with coke as a fuel and reducing agent and with limestone as a flux. The pig iron resulting from this process contains about 92-95 per cent iron together with some carbon, silicon, sulfur, phosphorus, and manganese.

The refining of steel from pig iron involves the reduction of the impurities in the pig iron. There are four steelmaking techniques. All of them use oxygen to oxidize the carbon, silicon, phosphorus, and manganese. The sulfur is removed by molten slag absorption.

The Bessemer process uses a largely enclosed converter vessel which contains the slag and the molten metal. Air is blown into the vessel over the metal. It is difficult to control for quality in the Bessemer process. Also this technique can not use scrap iron and emits large quantities of air pollutants.

The open hearth, which has dominated the steel making technologies most of this century, consists of a regenerative reverberating furnace in which a long, shallow bath is heated by radiation from a luminous flame. The fuel may be liquid petroleum gas, natural gas, coke oven gas, fuel oil, or coal tar. Of the four techniques the open hearth has the greatest flexibility in the mix of pig iron and scrap that it can use. Scrap may make up anywhere from 20 to 80 per cent of the charge. The greatest advantage of the open hearth is its ability to minimize costs of production by utilizing the optimum mix of scrap and hot metal in the charge.

The electric furnace technique usually consists of melting and refining a cold charge of steel scrap with electric power as a source of heat. Graphite electrodes transmit the current to the charge producing an arc the resistance of which generates heat for melting. The outstanding feature of the electric furnace is the high degree of process control. Almost any composition or grade of steel can be made in the electric furnace.

Much of the alloy steel is produced in electric furnaces. The cost of producing steel with the electric furnace depends on the price of electricity and scrap. Since electricity is generally a higher cost fuel than fossil fuels and since scrap prices are extremely volatile, the electric furnace is used largely to produce the higher valued alloy steels. Since the electric furnace starts with scrap, a blast furnace to produce the pig iron is not required. Thus the electric furnace is ideally suited for non-integrated steel companies.

The basic oxygen process consists of a converter vessel, either in a fixed upright position or rotary. After the furnace is charged with scrap and molten iron (usually 70 per cent hot metal and 30 per cent scrap) an oxygen lance is lowered to the bath surface. Pure oxygen is injected downward at a high velocity which causes chemical and physical reactions in the bath. Heat is produced by the oxidation of carbon, silicon, manganese, and phosphorus in the hot metal. The amount of heat generated is sometimes more than is needed. Then scrap is added as a coolant. Unlike the open hearth furnace, the basic oxygen furnace does not need external fuel. The basic oxygen furnace has several advantages over the open hearth, 1) lower energy requirements, 2) smaller capital investment, 3) less laber, and 4) much shorter heat time, 35-45 minutes as compared to 7-8 hours for an open hearth. As a result of these advantages, the B.O.F. is gradually replacing the open hearth furnace.

The next stage in the production of steel is the finishing mills. Here there are two alternative process, 1) conventional casting, and 2) continuous casting. At present 94 per cent of domestic raw steel is cast in the form if ingots which are preheated in soaking pits to a temperature of 2200-2400 degrees Fahrenheit prior to rolling on a slabbing or blooming mill. The continuous casting process on the other hand takes the hot molten steel directly from the steel furnace and casts the blooms and slabs. Since no preheating is required for this process, it uses less energy than conventional casting. Also continuous casting has a higher yield (95 per cent versus 86 per cent) than conventional casting, because less steel wastage is produced.

2.3 The Development of the Steel Making Technologies

Large scale steel making began when Bessemer and Kelly showed how to refine molten pig iron by blowing it with air in large vessels. In 1864 the first Bessemer converter was built in the United States. About this time Siemans in England and Martin in France showed how to use regenerative shallow bath furnaces to make steel from pig iron and scrap. This process became known as the open hearth process. The first open hearth furnace in the United States was built in 1870.

Use of the Bessemer process continued to grow in the United States until it reached 11 million tons in 1906. After this, Bessemer tonnage began to decline. By 1908 open hearth tonnage had surpassed

Bessemer tonnage and continued to grow until it was replaced by the B.O.F. in the 1960's. While it was cheaper to construct a Bessemer converter than an open hearth furnace, the Bessemer converter had two disadvantages, 1) the quality of Bessemer steel was not equal to that of open hearth steel, especially for sheets, and 2) the Bessemer converter could not use scrap whereas the open hearth could use a wide mix of pig iron and scrap. Another factor that would become important in the future was that the open hearth emitted fewer pollutants than the Bessemer.

The electric furnace was developed in France in 1901 by Heroult. The first electric furnace in the United States was built in 1906. It was primarily used to produce alloy steels and replaced the crucible furnace which previously had been used to produce alloy steel. The electric furnace has always had limited applications since 1) it can only consume scrap and 2) electricity is usually a more costly energy source than fossil fuels.

The B.O.F. was invented by Robert Durer in Switzerland in 1949. The first commercial B.O.F. went into operation in Austria in 1952. The first B.O.F. in the United States was installed by McLouth steel in 1954. The B.O.F. produces higher quality steel than the open hearth. The B.O.F. is also capital saving, labor saving, and energy saving compared to the open hearth furnace. For these reasons, the B.O.F. is rapidly replacing the open hearth furnace.

2.4 Comparison of the Rate of Diffusion of the B.O.F. in the U.S. and Japanese Steel Industries

The B.O.F. became a commercial reality with the VOEST Plant in Austria in June, 1952. In 1954 McLouth Steel Company became the first corporation in the United States to install a basic oxygen furnace. However its introduction was not the result of deliberate industrial planning. McLouth Steel Corporation in Trenton, Michigan was organized in 1934 for the purpose of processing steel slabs into hot rolled strip for the Detroit automobile industry. In 1947 the company was forced to integrate backwards when its steel slab supplier discontinued steel shipments. Thus it acquired four 60 ton electric furnaces. The major problems of the high cost of electricity and the dependence on an unstable scrap supply made operating costs difficult to control.

In 1952 General Motors, foreseeing a shortage in steel capacity for the late 1950's and doubtful that the steel industry would develop sufficient capacity to meet the auto industry's needs, had decided to finance the expansion of the capacity of four companies guaranteeing purchases on a percentage basis. One of those was McLouth steel. Part of those expansion plans involved constructing Bessemer converters, which would provide low quality steel at low capital costs to be added to the electric furnaces along with the scrap which could reduce the costs of operating the electric furnaces. However the Bessemer emitted large amounts of smoke which was forbidden by the town ordinances. McLouth was unable to effect a compromise with the town officials. Thus the only alternative, short of completely scrapping their plans for the Bessemer, was to install a smoke disposal unit and redesign the Bessemer converters into basic oxygen furnaces. In December, 1954 McLouth became the first company with a B.O.F. in the United States. Its 500,000 ton capacity also made it the largest B.O.F. in the world at the time. They found that the steel was of such high quality that it could be used without further refining. It was so successful that by 1960 they had installed two million tons of B.O.F. capacity. At the time McLouth was a medium sized producer making approximately one million tons annually.

Although the introduction of the B.O.F. into the United States by McLouth was somewhat accidental, the installation in November, 1957 of a B.O.F. by Jones and Laughlin Steel Corporation, one of the eight largest steel producers in the United States, was planned as a means of increasing tonnage more cheaply. Until 1960 it was the opportunity for cheaper expansion that lay behind all of the B.O.F. projects. It wasn't until 1961 that the steel industry began replacing existing open hearth with the B.O.F. By the end of the first decade after the introduction of the B.O.F. into the United States, large steel companies (the third through the eighth largest, excluding the two largest) accounted for 58 per cent of the total B.O.F. capacity while accounting for 35 per cent of total steel making capacity. The medium sized firms accounted for 42 per cent of total B.O.F. capacity (firms with a total capacity ranging between 1-2 per cent of total United States steel capacity) while taking 13 per cent of total steel making capacity. The two largest steel firms (U.S. Steel and

Bethlehem) did not install B.O.F.'s until 1964. U.S. Steel and Bethlehem opted to modernize their existing open hearth facilities rather than install new B.O.F.'s. However this strategy led, in part, to a loss of nine percentage points in the combined market share of U.S. Steel and Bethlehem which was picked up by the large and medium sized producers, i.e. by the companies that were the imitators. Thus the medium sized firms have been the industry leaders in adopting the new technology. The large firms have been relatively quick in adopting the B.O.F. While giant sized firms have been laggards, small firms have been non-adopters, most likely, because it has been more difficult for them to finance the replacement of the O.H. with the B.O.F.

While it is true that the two largest firms were slow in adopting the B.O.F., it does not necessarily follow that the industry as a whole was laggard in their diffusion of the B.O.F. as has been alleged. Japan's steel industry is often held up as an example of a steel industry with the most modern equipment having a high rate of diffusion of new technologies. Hence it would be useful to compare the United States and Japanese steel industries.

It has been stated one of the reasons that Japan was able to develop a modern steel industry so rapidly after the second world war was that Japan's steel industry was largely destroyed. However this was not true. Only 14 per cent of their steel making capacity was damaged by the war. The major differences were: 1) the rate of expansion of steel making capacity, 2) the method of financing of the expansion, and 3) the marketing strategy of the industry. After the war Japan had six million tons of productive capacity whereas the United States had 90 million tons. By 1960 Japan's capacity had grown to 25 million tons, an increase of over 400 per cent, while the capacity of the United States had grown to 149 million tons, an increase of only 166 per cent. And by 1976 Japan had 151 million tons, a 25 fold increase, while the United States had 159 million tons, an increase of only 177 per cent over 1946. Between 1960 and 1976 the United States added only ten million tons of capacity while Japan added 126 million. Thus, while the Japanese steel industry sustained a massive increase in their capacity, United States steel industry growth was moderate and leveled off after 1960.

Japan did not install its first B.O.F. until 1957 three years after the first B.O.F. had been installed in the United States. It was installed by Yawata, once of the six large steel companies which dominate Japan's steel industry with 75 per cent of the capacity. By 1971 Japan had a B.O.F. capacity of 74 million tons as compared to 70 million for the United States. In view of the fact that the United States had added only ten million tons of steel making capacity between 1971 and 1961, while Japan had added 80 million tons of capacity, it appears that when compared to Japan, the United States steel industry was not laggard in adopting the B.O.F. (see Table 1).

The method of financing new capacity plays an important role in determining the rate of expansion of the industry and thus its rate of adoption of new technologies. The Japanese government has played

Table 2.1

Steel Production and Capacity in the United States and Japan

	B.O.F.			O.H.			Elect. Furnace		
	Japan	U.S.		Japan	U.S.		Japan	U.S.	
	Prod.	Prod.	Cap.	Prod.	Prod.	Cap.	Prod.	Prod.	Cap.
1955	----	307	540	7,814	105,359	110,234	1,187	8,050	10,808
1956	----	506	540	8,967	102,841	112,316	1,691	8,641	10,719
1957	454	611	620	9,930	101,658	116,912	2,187	7,971	11,502
1958	826	1,323	1,479	9,211	75,880	122,321	2,081	6,656	13,312
1959	1,206	1,864	2,861	12,312	81,669	126,529	3,112	8,533	13,495
1960	2,629	3,346	4,155	15,045	86,368	126,622	4,464	8,379	14,397
1961	5,357	3,967	4,650	16,971	84,502	125,076	5,941	8,664	14,804
1962	8,441	5,553	7,500	13,285	82,957	123,531	5,821	9,013	15,211
1963	12,045	8,544	10,300	12,195	88,834	121,985	7,262	10,920	15,618
1964	17,581	15,442	15,960	13,853	98,098	120,441	8,365	12,678	16,049
1965	22,629	22,879	23,687	10,164	94,193	112,893	8,368	13,804	17,402
1966	29,921	33,928	34,738	8,635	85,025	105,345	9,237	14,870	18,454
1967	41,751	41,434	39,906	9,042	70,690	100,989	11,361	15,089	19,524
1968	49,281	48,812	49,813	5,424	65,836	91,492	12,188	16,814	20,695
1969	63,191	60,236	61,236	5,240	60,894	79,099	18,735	20,132	21,937
1970	73,847	63,330	66,429	3,855	48,022	72,818	15,620	20,162	23,253
1971	70,840	63,943	70,244	2,090	35,559	67,858	15,630	20,941	24,648

a key role in the modernization and expansion of industry. With respect to the coal and steel industries the government developed a program, 1) to insure the availability of sufficient funds for the development of the industries at low interest rates, 2) to grant preferential treatment in the importation of foreign machinery and technology, 3) to reduce the cost of coal, both imported and domestic, 5) to rationalize the transportation system and reduce its cost, 5) to insure the availability of scrap iron, 6) to guide the rationalization efforts of the two industries, and 7) to pursue a vigorous export oriented economy after the domestic economy had recovered from the effects of the war. For the period 1945-1955, government loan to industry accounted for 40 per cent of total investment capital with 11 per cent coming from commercial bank loans and 49 per cent coming from internal funds and the issuance of stocks and bonds. For the period 1956-60, 15 per cent came from Japanese government loans, 12 per cent from international agencies and foreign government loans, 14 per cent from commercial sources, and 64 per cent from internal sources and the issuances of stocks and bonds. Since 1960 government loans have largely been replaced by commercial loans with loans financing an increasing portion of industrial investment. Consequently steel industry debt was 83 per cent while equity was only 17 per cent in 1974. This contrasts with a 23 per cent debt to 77 per cent equity for the United States steel industry. The high Japanese debt to equity ratio comes about as a result of the fact that the central bank of Japan has allowed their commercial banks to maintain loan to deposit ratios of from 92 to 98 per cent whereas United States commercial bank loan to deposit ratios have ranged from 75-83 per cent. Thus the risk of investment, particularly, in new technologies has largely been taken over by the government. With the government absorbing some of the risk, the steel industry pursued a vigorous rate of expansion whereas the United Steel industry only expanded moderately.

Since much of the raw materials and energy required for the development of the Japanese economy had to be imported, it was necessary for Japan to export a significant portion of its production in order to maintain its balance of payments. Once the economy had recovered from the war, the Japanese government began a vigorous policy of encouraging exports. During the period 1957-66 exports accounted for 36 per cent of production growth while during the period 1967-76 exports accounted for 66 per cent of production growth. The United States government has not had a policy to encourage exports [1] and the steel industry has generally oriented its production for the domestic market.

There are other factors which enhanced the efficiency of the Japanese steel industry. Large multipurpose ships were developed to carry large quantities of imports to Japan and exports from Japan. This resulted, in part, in the reduction of the nominal c.i.f. price of iron ore declining from $16.70/ton in 1956 to $15.15/ton in 1975 while the c.i.f. price of iron ore paid by United States steel makers arose from $9.63/ton in 1956 to $23.99/ton in 1975. Likewise the gap in the cost of coking coal between the United States and Japan was narrowed during this period. The scarceness of land in Japan has tended to induce a more efficient layout of plant facilities thus encouraging the construction of integrated steel plants which in turn has induced the rapid adoption of the continuous casting technology. Central government land use planning also enabled the government to facilitate the location of steel mills at deepwater ports where the government also constructed port and rail facilities. This type of centralized land use and infrastructure planning does not exist in the United States.

Like the United States steel industry 15 years earlier, the Japanese steel industry appears to have reached its maturity [2]. It appears to have sufficient capacity for the next decade. South Korea, India, and South Africa have been challenging Japanese steel on the world market with lower prices primarily as a result of lower labor costs. If one takes as a hypothesis that the major determinant of the degree of innovation and adoption of new technologies by an industry is the degree to which it is still a young and growing industry, under intense competition, (not necessarily among the individual firms in the national industry), then it will be interesting to see if Japan can maintain the modern efficient character of its steel industry while under still competition from young and growing industries of some of the LDC's. This hypothesis is more reminiscent of Schumpeters' doctrine of creative destruction rather than Mansfield's "micro" hypothesis on inter-firm innovation and immitation. Gold, Peirce, and Rosegger [3] find that when rates of diffusion are compared against growth rates of "old" and "new" output the results are ambiguous. They show that a high rate of growth does not necessarily insure a high rate of diffusion of a new technology and vice versa. However they do not include the degree of competition as an explanatory variable. Clearly the decision making process in industry is very complex and can not be fully explained by two or three variables. However the rate of growth of the industry and degree of competition should be included as major explanatory variables in any model unless shown not to be significant. In the dynamic portion of our model we have used the quantity of imports as a proxy for the degree of international competition. Also the growth of the industry is included as an explanatory variable.

References

1. Business Week, April 10, 1978, p. 54.

2. Business Week, January 30, 1978, p. 44, and The Wall Street Journal, December 7, 1977, p. i.

3. Gold, Peirce, and Rosegger, "Diffusion of Major Technological Innovations in U.S. Iron and Steel Manufacturing", Journal of Industrial Economics, July, 1970.

Chapter III

The Aluminum Industry

3.1 Introduction

In order to understand technological change in the aluminum industry, it is important to study the development of the industry. The task of refining pure aluminum from aluminum bearing ores has been long and arduous. Reducing electricity consumption by the aluminum refining process still remains one of the major goals of the industry. Unlike steel, the aluminum industry has had to develop markets for its products which has served to induce technological change in other industries, notably the metal cans industry.

3.2 Development of the Technology

Aluminum has been used for thousands of years in the form of aluminum bearing clays used for pottery. Certain other aluminum compounds such as alums were widely used by the Egyptians and Babylonians as early as 2000 B.C. in vegetable dyes, chemical processes, and medicines. It was not until the 19th century, however, that pure aluminum was produced. The major obstacle was the strong bond between the aluminum and oxygen. In 1825 Oersted produced a small lump of aluminum by heating potassuim amalgam with aluminum chloride and found aluminum embedded with the amalgam. Successive advances in the chemical process for refining aluminum reduced the price of aluminum to $8 a pound by the 1860's which made the commercial development of the aluminum industry feasible. Its cost, however, was still too high for widespread use. In 1886, Hall and Heroult working independently discovered a workable electrolytic process. Most aluminum is still refined by this method. Although they both used batteries as their source of electricity, it was the recent invention of the dynamo and thus large scale generation of electric power that made their process the commercial success that it has become. The commercialization further reduced the price of aluminum so that by the early 1900's it had dropped below 30 cents per pound. While the search for improved alumina reduction techniques has tended to dominate research activities in the aluminum industry, other aspects of the industry have been improved through research. About two years after the discovery of the electrolytic process for alumina reduction, Bayer found an improved process for making pure aluminum oxide from low-silica-content bauxite ores. Productivity in the alumina reduction facilities nearly doubled between 1950 and 1972. This was accomplished by using larger reduction cells with better thermal characteristics and by more careful control of operating conditions of individual cells.

In 1972 Alcoa announced that it had developed a new process for process for producing primary aluminum. Alumina is reacted with chlorine to form aluminum chloride which is electrolyzed in a closed cell to produce molten aluminum metal and chlorine. The chlorine is then recycled. The process operates at lower temperatures than present cells which are based on a bath containing fluoride. The new process uses 30 per cent less electricity, less labor, and requires less space. It also eliminates the need to contain fluoride emissions. A 15,000 ton per year facility to determine the commercial potential of the process has been constructed.

3.3 The Structure of the Industry

The Pittsburg Reduction Company was founded in 1888 by Hall and a group of investors in order to commercialize the Hall process. In 1907 the company changed its name to the Aluminum Company of America (Alcoa). Throughout the world the growth of the aluminum industry was the growth of Alcoa. It was the only large aluminum producer until after World War II. In 1937 Alcoa was charged with monopolization. The legal process had not been completed by the start of the war. After the war, other companies entered the market (Kaiser and Reynolds) and all charges against Alcoa were dropped. At present Alcoa has about one-third of the market. Alcoa, Reynolds, and Kaiser dominate the aluminum ingot industry with about 80 per cent of the market.

3.4 Development of the Market for Aluminum

One of the problems that Hall and his company faced was the need to develop markets for aluminum. This has consisted of promoting aluminum as a substitute for steel, wood, and copper, and developing new products which used aluminum. Until recently, however, the high cost of aluminum relative to steel and wood has made it generally unacceptable as a substitute for these materials. Thus for the aluminum industry to grow, a vigorous cost reduction program was necessary. This consisted of research to reduce the high electrical energy requirements which account for 16 per cent of the total cost of producing aluminum and to develop the ability to use non-bauxite low-aluminum content ores. The price of aluminum has fallen dramatically since 1900. In 1950 the real price of aluminum was one-fifth of what it was in 1900. Since then its price has remained relatively stable. Alcoa executives have explicitly stated that their goal has been to keep the price trend down in order to broaden the market [1]. This is a long run pricing policy. Peck [2] demonstrates that the market price of aluminum ingot bears little relation to the current supply and demand situation. In contrast to the steel industry, the aluminum industry has been involved in the manufacture and the development of the machinery for the production of finished products. None of the steel companies manufacture cans whereas Kaiser Aluminum and Reynolds not only manufacture the cans, but Kaiser furthermore developed the two-piece beverage can manufacturing machinery. This has resulted in aluminum cans capturing 63 per cent of the beer market and 18 per cent of the soft drink market by 1970. However by 1971 the steel industry had developed thin steel plate suitable for use in the two-piece machinery and had started to make a come back. This competition between the two metals has tended to keep down the price of the metal can stock. During the years 1975 and 1976 the price of aluminum ingot rose 95 per cent and the average price of all steel products rose

56 per cent. By contrast, the price of aluminum can stock has remained fixed and tinplates' price has dropped by two per cent [3]. However in May, 1978 Alcoa announced it was going to raise its price of aluminum can stock. It was going to concentrate on making its can stock more profitable rather than trying to expand their share of the beverage can market.

Both aluminum and steel producers use their sheet products as a means of stabilizing output in their respective industries. While production of many steel and aluminum products is subject to the fluctuations of the business cycle, production in the beverage industry is not significantly affected by the business cycle. Cans account for about 13 per cent of total aluminum output and 10 per cent of steel.

Competition between aluminum and other materials has been intense. In the 1950's aluminum largely replaced copper in electrical power transmission lines. Aluminum is increasingly replacing steel in automobiles. This process will be accelerated as automobile manufacturers are forced to lighten their vehicles. However plastic may take some of aluminum's share of the automobile market. The competition between aluminum and steel in aircraft has been intense during the past three decades. Initially, aluminum replaced steel as the skin for aircraft. Then, as strong thin steels were developed, they again replaced aluminum. About 20 per cent of all aluminum production goes to the transportation sector. Aluminum has recently gained an advantage over tinplate and plastics because of the relative ease with which it is recycled and because of the large difference in the cost of using aluminum scrap versus virgin aluminum. This means that recycled aluminum can command a higher price than steel scrap which tends to encourage recycling of aluminum. This would also give aluminum cans an advantage over steel cans.

3.5 The Future of the Aluminum Industry

The era of cheap electricity for the production of aluminum has ended. Already new aluminum reduction facilities are being planned away from the traditional regions (Pacific Northwest and Southeast) where cheap power was available. These new facilities will be located in the region where their markets are found. This will result in the decentralization of aluminum production. Also there will be a shift of new facilities to areas where energy is currently cheap such as the Middle East, Northern Africa, and Southern Europe. Some of the countries that are exporters of bauxite will be producing their own aluminum for export thereby capturing the increased value added. This process will be hastened if and when a direct reduction process which bypasses the alumina stage is developed. Since it is alumina rather than the bauxite that is increasingly being exported, all of these developments would tend to limit the expansion of the alumina industry in the United States. It will be interesting to see what effect these developments will have on the rate of adoption of the new chlorine reduction process.

References

1. House Committee on the Judiciary, Hearings: Study of Monopoly Power, Serial No. 1, Part 1, Aluminum, 1951, pp. 632-678.
2. Peck, Morton, Competition in the Aluminum Industry, Harvard University Press, Cambridge, 1961, p. 56.
3. Business Week, November 22, 1976, p. 78.

Chapter IV

The Can Manufacturing Industry

4.1 Introduction

In order to understand technological change in the metal can industry, it is necessary to study the development of the industry along with the can making process. The competition for the container market between various materials has also had an impact on the development of the can manufacturing industry. The ease with which cans can be manufactured by canners also has affected technological change in the metal can industry.

4.2 Can Making Technology

Although the three-piece technology for making cans has long dominated the industry, the development of the two-piece technology during the past two decades has made possible the use of aluminum as a material for cans. The three-piece can consists of two ends and a cylindrical body. The ends and the can body are cut from a sheet of tinplate. The body piece is formed and the seam is either soldered, cemented, or welded. Then the bottom end is soldered, cemented, or welded to the can body. As many as 800 three-piece cans can be produced in a minute. Although most three-piece can lines run between 500-600 cans per minute. If the label is to be lithographed on the body of the can, it would be done on the sheets from which the bodies are cut.

The impact extrusion technology was developed in the late 1950's by Kaiser Aluminum as a means of providing new markets in the beverage container market for its aluminum plate. In this process an aluminum slug made of soft high purity metal and resembling an oversized silver dollar is fed into a die recess and struck sharply with a can shaped punch. This forces the metal to flow out of the die upward along the punch into a can shape. The rough shell is then trimmed, flanged, cleaned, coated, and printed. This process was used to make 8 oz. beer cans. The inability to control the thickness uniformly on the can rendered it uneconomic for larger sizes. More metal is left on the body than is required. In the early 1960's the draw and iron (D & I) technology was perfected for use with aluminum cols. A coil is fed into a cupping press where a disc is blanked out and drawn into a cup. The cup is then fed into a draw and iron press where it is drawn to the final diameter. The iron and draw process may be repeated in a redraw operation to reduce the diameter of the cup and reduce the thickness of the wall. In the draw and iron process one can use strong tempered aluminum alloys which allows for thinner walls and thus lighter and cheaper cans. The D & I process uses 10-12 per cent less aluminum than the impact extrusion method. The D & I technology has replaced the impact extrusion technology which only had limited applications. In 1971 the D & I technology was adapted for use with thin steel plate. With the draw and iron technology, as many as 2000 cans per minute can be produced. Two-piece D & I 12 oz. steel beverage cans weigh 101 lbs/1000 cans whereas three-piece tinplate cans weigh 122 lbs/1000 cans. The three-piece technology used for making beverage cans is rapidly either being scrapped or shipped to third world countries.

4.3 Development of the Can Making Technologies

Although the art of coating iron with tin was known and practiced prior to 25 A.D., the first tinplate reportedly was to have been made in Bohemia around 1240. It appears that the process was kept secret until the seventeenth century when tinplate production was begun in England.

The quest for a better container, which led to the development of the tin can, was probably started by Napolean's offer of 12,000 francs for a method of preserving food to sustain his army. In 1809 a Parisian chef, Nicolas Appert, won the award for his new process of canning. A year later Peter Durand invented the "tin canister" incorporating the canning process developed by Appert. When William Underwood migrated from England to Boston in 1817, he brought this process with him and started the canning industry in the United States. Until the 1900's cans were made slowly by hand. Both ends were soldered to the can with a hole about an inch in diameter in the top. After filling the can through this hole, a tinplate disk was soldered in place.

The "sanitary style" open-top can was introduced in the early 1900's. This type of construction made it possible to develop high-speed equipment for making, filling and closing these cans. The original had made csns were produced at the rate of five or six per hour, but modern machines can produce as many as 2000 cans per minute.

After the development of the sanitary can, few changes took place until World War II. Although the electrolytic tinplate process, which made possible the reduction of the tin content of the tinplate, became commercial in 1937, it was not until World War II that the tin content was actually reduced as a result of the rationing of tin. The tin content was reduced from one pound/basebox to one-half pounds per basebox. In the early 1950's with 45 per cent of the world's production of tin coming from Asia, which at the time was not considered a secure source of raw materials, the major can companies undertook an intensive program to reduce the dependency on tin. This took the form of further reducing the tin content of the tin plate and developing tin free steel plate. During the 1950's much of the research on tin free steels was done by the can manufacturers rather than the steel companies. It wasn't until the 1960's that the steel companies, under intense competitive pressure from aluminum, undertook the development of tin free steel plates. No universal coating has been found that will resist corrosion from any substance in the container. A variety of coatings have been developed which are corrosion resistant to specific substances.

While aluminum had been used for fish cans, it had not been used on a large scale. In the 1950's aluminum companies developed aluminum alloys that were sufficiently hardened to withstand easy denting and the pressures required for canning beer and soda. Kaiser Aluminum also adapted the impact extrusion technology for making 8 oz. beer cans which it then leased to Coors. The impact extrusion technology was not suited for making 12 oz. cans, which is the dominant can in the industry, since too much aluminum was required as a result of the thick bottom, which it produced, thus making it too costly. In the early 1960's the draw and iron technology was developed which enabled them to manufacture a uniformly thin walled container. Since the D & I two-piece technology produced cans much cheaper than the conventional three-piece can and since the aluminum can was much lighter than the three-piece tinplate can, it soon captured a significant portion of the beer and soda can market. In the late 1960's the steel industry developed some tinplate and tin free steel plate for use with the two-piece technology. The first two-piece steel plate line went into operation in 1971. Currently there is heavy competition between aluminum and steel for the beer and soda can market [2].

While the first beer and soda cans were produced in 1935, production remained small until after World War II. Sales of canned beer were buoyed by the changing nature of beer consumption. Before World War II most beer was consumed in bars and restaurants in bulk form or in bottles. After the war more beer was consumed in the home where the preferred container was the can, since it was lighter and would not break.

Plastic beer and soda bottles were recently introduced but were withdrawn after PCV contaimination of the contents of the bottles was discovered. If plastic bottles are reintroduced, it is expected that they will replace glass bottles rather than cans.

Nearly every type of material has been used at one time or another for frozen orange juice cans. The frozen orange juice market developed after World War II. Initially they were packaged in tinplate cans. In the late 1950's the aluminum can for frozen orange juice was developed and tended to replace the tinplate can because it was lighter. Around 1960 the composite can was developed. It consists of a fiber body with metal ends. Since the composite can was both lighter and cheaper it replaced the metal can. Recently some frozen juice has been packaged in plastic containers. Thus far they have not replaced the composite can and it is not clear that they will since the weight difference is not that great. Cost data are not available (only Tropicana is using the plastic can).

There has been virtually no change in the technology or materials used in the manufacture of vegetable and fruit cans. The tin content has been reduced and the thickness of the plate and the weight of the can have been reduced significantly. Aluminum has not been able to replace tinplate since it must have sufficient rigidity in order to withstand denting and must be able to withstand the cooking temperatures required for the canning of the fruit and vegetables. In canned beverages, internal pressure from the carbonation is sufficient to prevent a thin aluminum or steel can from denting too easily.

4.4 The Structure of the Industry

The dominant firm in the can manufacturing industry has been the American Can Company. It was organized in 1901 in order to bring the entire can industry under the control of a single trust. The company did not maintain the position of monopoly that its organizers had expected. From a peak of over 90 per cent of industry sales in 1901 the share of American fell rapidly to about 50 per cent of industry sales in 1913. This reduction in market share may have come about intentionally as a means of avoiding a dissolution of the company, similar to the Standard Oil case. This decline in market share was one of the principle reasons for the court's decision not to order the dissolution of the company. After the 1916 antitrust decision, American Can changed from being a high price and restriction minded trust to one with an emphasis on product improvement and market expansion. Until the 1960's its market share had remained stable with between 40-50 per cent of the market.

Continental Can Company was organized in 1904 during the period when American Can was holding prices so high that the entry of new firms was encouraged. By 1919 Continental had become the second largest firm in the industry with around 10 per cent of the market. By 1939 Continental had 25 per cent of the of the total can market.

In 1972 American had 26 per cent of the market, Continental had 23 per cent of the market, Reynolds had 10 per cent, and Kaiser had 3 per cent. It appears that Reynolds and Kaiser have taken some of American's share of the market. The top eight manufacturers had 79 per cent of the market which indicates that the structure of the can manufacturing industry is still oligopolistic.

Both American and Continental have diversified into other packaging lines (e.g. bottles, fibre board containers, boxes, packaging material, etc.). It has only been within the past decade that they have diversified into non-packaging lines with Continental buying insurance companies along with its timber, paper mill, and printing presses and American buying magazines, garment patterns, etc. Both companies have also expanded their packaging operations outside the United States. Continental earned 30 per cent of its profits abroad in 1975 and American earned 13 per cent abroad. With the advent of the aluminum beverage can, American and Continental faced stiff competition from Kaiser Aluminum and Reynolds which not only marketed the Aluminum coil but also manufactured the cans. American and Continental now manufacture both steel and aluminum cans.

While the can manufacturing industry is highly concentrated, there is one factor that tends to inhibit monopoly pricing, namely the possibility of self-manufacture. The barriers to entry are not very restrictive. Many of the larger canners manufacture a portion of their own cans. The cost of installing a canning line is relatively low, and the requirements of economics of scale are not severe. Some can manufacturers have gone to great lengths to initiate arrangements so favorable with the canner that it would not be in the interest of the canner to manufacture their own cans. Continental can retained its business with the Campbell Soup Company by offering Campbell low prices and maintained an efficient factory next door to the Campbell plant. It has been estimated that in the early 1930's the Campbell account represented 30 per cent of Continental's output of packers cans. The passage of the Robinson-Patman Act eliminated this type of arrangement and Campbell eventually acquired the can manufacturing plant from Continental. Heinz and Hunt are among the larger canners which manufacture a portion of their own cans. In the late 1950's both Minutemaid and Coors began making their own aluminum cans. Coors was one of the pioneers in using the two-piece technology.

In recent years the competition between aluminum and steel for the can market has kept down the price of the can stock of both metals. Both the aluminum and steel companies use their production of can stock as a means of stabilizing their output. Consequently their production lines tend to run at capacity with expansion being undertaken reluctantly. Thus the demand for can stock on occasion tends to outstrip the supply. Thus far no can manufacturing company has integrated upstream though some have investigated the possibility.

References

1. A basebox consists of 112 sheets with each sheet 14" x 20".

2. Business Week, November 22, 1976, p. 78.

Chapter V

A Recursive Programming Model of Investment and Technological Change in an Input-Output Framework

5.1 Introduction

Recursive programming can be characterized as a dynamic input-output structure with multiple production processes. A recursive program is composed of two distinct phases (1) the static linear program, (2) the dynamic recursive feedback mechanism and behavioral relationships. The model consists of a sequence of linear programs of which, (a) the objective function, and primary input and final demand constraints depend on various exogenous variables, (b) the capital limitations depend on past capital stocks, depreciation rates, and the investment levels determined by the preceeding linear program problem in the sequence, and (c) current investment constraints depend on past accumulations of capital and on expected final demand. The model is run by (1) taking the initial period's conditions as given, (2) solving the first period's linear program, (3) updating the endogenous and exogenous constraints and cost parameters, and (4) solving the succeeding period's linear program, etc.

Recursive programming models were developed by Day [2]. While the methodology of recursive programming is but one among several dynamic input-output structures with multiple production process, its unique contribution is the inclusion of an optimizing criterion while at the same time allowing for behavioral interaction and environmental feedback within the dynamic structure.

Day and his students have used recursive programming models to study industries with multiple processes, e.g. coal, steel, etc. They have not used the model to study the interaction of many distinct industries, although Day does indicate that this would be a natural extension of his work [2]. We will be focusing on the dominant process in each of the industries, the steel making process (the steel furnace) in the steel industry, the aluminum reduction process in the aluminum industry, and the can manufacturing process in the metal can industry.

5.2 The Recursive Programming Model

The primal recursive programming problem is summarized as follows:

$$\theta(t) = \min \left[\sum_{i=1}^{m} \hat{P}_i(t) x_i(t) + \sum_{j=1}^{n} \hat{\rho}_j(t) y_j(t) \right]$$

subject to

(1) $-z_j(t) \leq -d_j(t) \qquad j = 1, \ldots\ldots, n$

(2) $-x_i(t) + \sum_{j=1}^{n} a_{ij}(t) z_j(t) \leq 0 \qquad i = 1, \ldots\ldots, m$

(3) $z_j(t) - y_j(t) \leq k(t-1) \qquad j = 1, \ldots\ldots, n$

(4) $x_i(t) \leq q_i(t) \qquad i = 1, \ldots\ldots, m$

(5) $y_j(t) + k_j(t-1) \leq k_j(t) \qquad j = 1, \ldots\ldots, n$

plus the requirement that all activity levels are non-negative.

Where,

p_i price of the output of the ith industry

x_i variable ith input

ρ_j marginal cost of capital in the jth industry

a_{ij} quantity of output of ith industry required to produce one unit of output of jth industry

d_i final demand for output of ith industry

y_i level of investment in capacity in the jth industry (given in units of annual capacity)

k_j total capacity of jth industry

z_j activity level of jth industry

q_i total supply of ith industry goods

The recursive feedback mechanism and behavioral relationships associated with the primal problem consists of the following:

A. Final Demand Forecast

$$\hat{d}_j(t) = F(p_j, p_j^I, d_j(t-1), \ldots\ldots, d_j(0), \hat{x}_i(t)) \qquad j \quad 1, \ldots, n$$

i - industry that is a consumer of jth industry output.

B. Technological Change

$$\bar{k}_l^j(t) = h\left[R_l^i(t),\ T_l^i, \mathrm{Prod}_l^i(t-1),\ k_l^i(t-1),\ \mathrm{Imp}_l(t-1),\ \gamma\right]_{i=1,\ \ldots,\ s}$$

$j = 1, \ldots, s$

$l = 1, \ldots, n$

C. The Cash-Flow Payoff Principle

$$\rho_j(t) = \gamma_j(t)\left[\frac{1}{\tau_j} - \frac{1}{\lambda_j}\right]$$

D. Forecasting Rules for Supplies

$$\hat{q}_i(t) = F_q(q_i(t-1),\ q_i(t-2) \ \ldots,\ q_i(t_0))$$

E. Capital Stock Identity

$$k_j(t) = y_j(t-1) + (1-\delta_j)k_j(t-1)$$

where,

δ_j rate of depreciation in the jth industry

k_l^j capacity with jth technology in the lth industry

T_l^i time interval separating the year when the first unit of capacity in the lth industry with ith technology was introduced in the United States

Imp_l imports of comparable goods produced by the lth industry

r interest rate

$prod_l^i$ output of lth commodity with the ith technology

γ_j total outlay per unit of investment in the jth industry

τ_j payoff period

λ_j life of project

P_l^I price of imports of lth commodity (comparable to output of lth industry)

R_l^i cost of producing the lth commodity with the ith technology

The dual recursive programming problem is summarized as follows:

$$\emptyset(t) = \max\left[- \sum_{j=1}^{n} \sigma_j k_j(t-1) - \omega L - \sum_{i=1}^{m} \nu_i q_i - \sum_{j=1}^{n} \eta_j \bar{y}_j(t) + \sum_{j=1}^{n} \psi_j d_j\right]$$

Subject to

$$\psi_j - \sum_{i=1}^{m} a_{ij}\mu_i - \sigma_j - \omega \leq 0 \qquad j = 1, \ldots, n$$

$$\mu_i - \nu_i \leq \hat{p}_i \qquad i = 1, \ldots, m$$

$$\sigma_j - \eta_j \leq \hat{\rho}_j \qquad j = 1, \ldots, n$$

$\nu_i, \mu_i \geq 0 \qquad i = 1, \ldots, n$

$\psi_j, \sigma_j, \eta_j \geq 0 \quad j = 1, \ldots, n$

$\omega \geq 0$

where,

μ_i imputed value per unit of the ith variable input (purchaser)

σ_j imputed value per unit of the capacity of the jth industry

ω imputed value per unit of labor

ν_i imputed value per unit of the ith variable input (supply level)

η_j imputed value per unit of the maximum potential investment in the jth capacity

ψ_j imputed value per unit of the jth final product.

Our primal problem minimizes the total cost of production and investment. The first constraint requires that the demand for the products be not greater than the output of that industry. The demand is determined during the recursive phase. The second constraint requires that the supplies of inputs must be greater than the interindustry demand. The interindustry demand is determined by the technical coefficients plus the quantity of the product to be produced. Since we are working in physical units, the technical coefficients are given in physical units. The third constraint is the capacity constraint. It states that total production of the jth industry at time t must be not greater than the capacity (given in units of outputs) at time $t-1$ plus investment in new capacity at time t. The fourth constraint is the primary input supply constraint. The value of $q_i(t)$ is determined during the recursive phase. The fifth constraint is the investment constraint. $\bar{y}_j(t)$ is determined by the maximum potential growth principle during the recursive phase.

During the recursive phase the constraints are updated. The marginal cost of capital is computed for the next period. Also during the recursive phase we estimate the demand for domestically produced inputs by industry. This is a function of the domestic price of the input, import price of the input, prices of close substitutes, demand for the input in previous periods, and expected output by industries using the input during the next period. The level of capacity of each technology for every industry is determined during the recursive phase. It is given by the technological change equation. We distinguish two phases of investment decisions. The first phase is the selection of projects from a number of alternative investment possibilities. This is the question of the marginal profitability of capital and the marginal cost of capital. The second phase is the determination of an upper limit on the level of investment in the projects in addition to the marginal investment criteria developed for the first phase. This is the problem of capital rationing operating in an environment of uncertainty and technological change.

The three common methods of project selection are (1) the present value approach, (2) the internal rate of return approach, and (3) the payoff approach. Let $\Omega_p(P)$ be the set of feasible solutions for the primal problem and $\Omega_d(D)$ the set of feasible solutions for the dual problem. Let $E = \{P \in R^M / \Omega_p(P) \neq \emptyset\}$

$F = \{D \in R^N / \Omega_d(D) \neq \emptyset\}$ and for $(P, D) \in E \times F$ define

$$M(P,D) = \min\{P'X/X \in \Omega_p(P)\} = \max\{\Lambda'D/\Lambda \in \Omega_d(D)\}$$

Then $\frac{\partial M(P,D)}{\partial k_j} = -\sigma_j$ provided the derivative exists. This means that the reduction in cost resulting from a one unit addition to the capacity of the jth industry is the same as the imputed value (quasi-rent) of the capacity. Thus one could rank all such projects (the addition of one unit of capacity) according to its imputed value and this value becomes a measure of the marginal profitability of capital.

The most common investment decision rule in business is some form of short term payback requirement [3; Ch. 9]. Usually management will specify that no investment outlay will be under taken unless it is expected to generate earnings that will return the initial investment outlay within a certain period of time i.e. three or five years.

Assume that the project under consideration will produce a known uniform flow of annual earnings over its lifetime, i.e. the marginal profitability of capital $\sigma_j(t)$ which is the imputed value derived above. Thus if the total outlay per unit of investment is represented by γ_j, the payoff period τ_j is expressed as

$$\tau_j(t) = \frac{\gamma_j(t)}{\sigma_j} \quad \text{or} \quad \sigma_j(t) = \frac{\gamma_j(t)}{\tau_j}$$

At equilibrium the marginal profitability of capital will be equal to the marginal cost of capital $\rho_j(t)$

$$\therefore \quad \rho_j(t) = \frac{\gamma_j(t)}{\tau_j}$$

where τ_j is now the equilibrium payoff period. Usually management will specify the maximum payoff period they are willing to consider. As a control device, the specified period may be less than the optimal period.

The most common form of payoff in business is the cash-flow payoff period [4; 229]. By cash-flow we mean profit net of all current out-of-pocket costs and taxes but not depreciation costs. This type of payoff provides a direct measure of the speed with which the capital outlay is recovered.

Assuming straight line depreciation, the cash-flow payoff period is

$$\tau_j = \frac{\gamma_j(t)}{\sigma_j(t) + \frac{\gamma_j(t)}{\lambda_j}}$$

where λ_j is the life of the project in years as determined by the IRS depreciation guidelines which we will use in the model. $\frac{\gamma_j(t)}{\lambda_j}$ is the annual depreciation cost per unit. At equilibrium $\sigma_j(t) = \rho_j(t$

$$\therefore \quad \rho_j(t) = \gamma_j(t) \left[\frac{1}{\tau_j^*} - \frac{1}{\lambda_j} \right]$$

where τ_j^* is the maximum payoff period the business is willing to consider.

The second phase of the investment decision is to determine the total amount to be invested in new plant and equipment in addition to the marginal analysis developed above. Capital rationing is imposed on the model because of imperfect foresight into the future, risk, and uncertainty. Although our model is non-stochastic, we attempt to take this into account through the use of the "maximum growth principle" which was originally formulated by Day [4; Ch. 5].

Day's version of the "maximum growth principle" is composed of two parts (1) the rate of adoption hypothesis, (2) the investment adjustment hypothesis. The rate of adoption hypothesis which assumes the adoption of a new technology follows a geometric growth curve and takes that curve to be an upperbound on investment in that new technology. This holds even if there is more than one new technology. to be diffused in the industry. The rate of adoption hypothesis requires that the upper bound of investment for each technology be determined separately with the linear programming part of the model determining the actual investment for that technology. Nelson [5] used this hypothesis in his recursive programming model of the steel industry in the United States. His model was interregional with the United States dissaggregated into 15 regions. He also separates the various processes required to produce a steel good from iron ore (blast furnace, steel furnace, rolling mill, etc.) and the basic steel forms that are final products of the industry. Despite this high degree of dissaggregation of the steel industry he was unable to estimate adequately the rate of adoption of the basic oxygen furnace and the electric furnace in the industry. Since it is our intent to model each industry as an aggregate, we believe that if we used the adoption hypothesis, our results would be even worse than Nelson's results. Thus we have followed an alternative procedure for introducing the rate of adoption of new technologies in the model. We estimate the rate of adoption by the technological change equations (B1). This gives us the total capacity of the particular technology we are examining.

The actual level of investment in a particular technology for a given period t_0 is computed by subtracting the estimated capacity in that technology at the beginning of t_0 from the estimated capacity at the beginning of the next period t_1. Since our model is highly aggregated, we cannot determine the actual level of investment during the static phase. What we do obtain during the static part is the level of utilization of the particular technology. This is actually what we are interested in obtaining as we wish to use this result to compute the technical coefficients for the industry. Based on Mansfield's studies [15] of the rate of diffusion of new technologies in industry, the level of investment in capacity of a particular technology, as given by the technological change equation, is a function of the cost of producing the good with this technology relative to the cost of producing it with other technologies, the cost of investing in additional capacity in the technology relative to other technologies, the capacity in that technology during previous periods, the vintage of the total capacity, the interest rate, the level of imports or production of close substitutes, and the level of production in that industry during the previous period.

The level of investment in capacity of a particular technology is determined during the dynamic phase rather than during the static phase. One can justify this approach by noting that the decision to expand capacity with a particular technology is made in advance, perhaps several years, of the time the financing for the expansion is actually obtained. To change to an alternate technology would require further planning, even if one takes into account that a certain amount of preliminary planning for alternate technologies would have gone into initial studies that led to the decision to choose a specific technology. In the short run the decision to invest in a particular technology is quite firm. While it is possible to cancel or alter investment in a specific technology, it is unlikely that this would be done after the equipment is in the process of being installed. Most likely this new capacity, although installed, would not be brought on line until it is anticipated that it will be needed. The decision to invest in a certain level of new capacity would not be made in the short run, i.e. during the static phase. What is decided in the short run is the amount of new capacity to bring on line, i.e. the level of new capacity to be utilized.

5.3 Application of the Model

The industries we are studying are the steel industry (SIC 331), the primary aluminum industry (SIC 3334), and metal cans (SIC 3411). The j subscripts in the model refer to these producing industries, where in this case n is 3. The energy and materials used by the above industries and consequently the particular technical coefficients we are examining are coal (SIC 12), gas utilities (SIC 492), electric utilities (SIC 491), petroleum refining products (SIC 2911), and iron ore (SIC 1011) for the steel industry; electric utilities, nonferrous ores (SIC 103), for the aluminum industries; steel and aluminum for the metal cans industry. These inputs are represented by the i subscripts in the model.

References

1. Mansfield, Edwin, Industrial Research and Technological Innovation, An Econometric Analysis, Norton & Co., Inc., New York, 1968.

2. Day, R.H., "Recursive Programming Models of Industrial Development and Technological Change", in A.P. Carter and A. Brody (eds.), Input-Output Techniques Vol. I, North-Holland, Amsterdam, 1970.

3. Smith, Vernon L., Investment and Production, Harvard University Press, Cambridge, 1961.

4. Day, R.H., Recursive Programming and Production Response, North-Holland, Amsterdam, 1963.

5. Nelson, Jon P., An Interregional Recursive Programming Model of the U.S. Iron and Steel Industry: 1947-1967, University of Wisconsin, Ph.D. Dissertation, 1970.

Chapter VI

Results and Evaluation

6.1 General Discussion

While we were working with three industries of the economy, only two were treated dynamically. Since there were no major innovations in aluminum refining during the period investigated, which was our major reason for developing a dynamic model, there was no point in estimating the equations for the dynamic part of the model. In the aluminum sector the constraints for the static part were given exogenously.

Since the steel sector was more complex than the others with the interplay of four steel making technologies and since regional data was available, the steel sector was divided into four regions. This enabled us to capture regional differences in raw material and energy costs, and in capacity constraints for the four steel making technologies. We modeled the period 1947-67 and attempted to forecase the period 1968-72.

As a comparison, a static version of the model, i.e. all constraints given exogenously, was run. The results of this model are found in the appendix.

Some of the independent variables in the equations of the dynamic phase, as described in Chapter V, do not appear in the equations actually estimated for specific industries and technologies. Variables in some instances were not significant or had to be eliminated because of multicollinearity problems. It was not possible to use both the total cost of using a technology and its capital cost as a result of multicollinearity. Since the decision makers usually consider the total cost to be a more important factor than the capital cost, only the total cost was used. In the initial attempt to estimate the equation, all of the relevant variables were used. Then the equation was again estimated using only those variables that were significant and not multicollinear with other variables. The coefficients and statistics of the equations presented below are those for the dependent variable regressed against only the significant and non-multicollinear independent variables.

6.2 Steel Sector

6.2.1 Dynamic Phase

The estimate of the demand for steel products is given by the final demand forecast equation:

$$\frac{SD}{XM} = \underset{(2.1)}{47.2} + \underset{(1.7)}{46.3}\ \frac{P_{IMP}}{P_{DOM}} + \underset{(2.3)}{0.5}\ \frac{SD_{-1}}{XM_{-1}} + \epsilon$$

R^2 is 0.62, F Statistic is 13.6. The Durbin-Watson Statistic is 2.2 which means there is no positive autocorrelation.

SD - demand for steel

XM - index of manufacturing production

Fig. 6.1

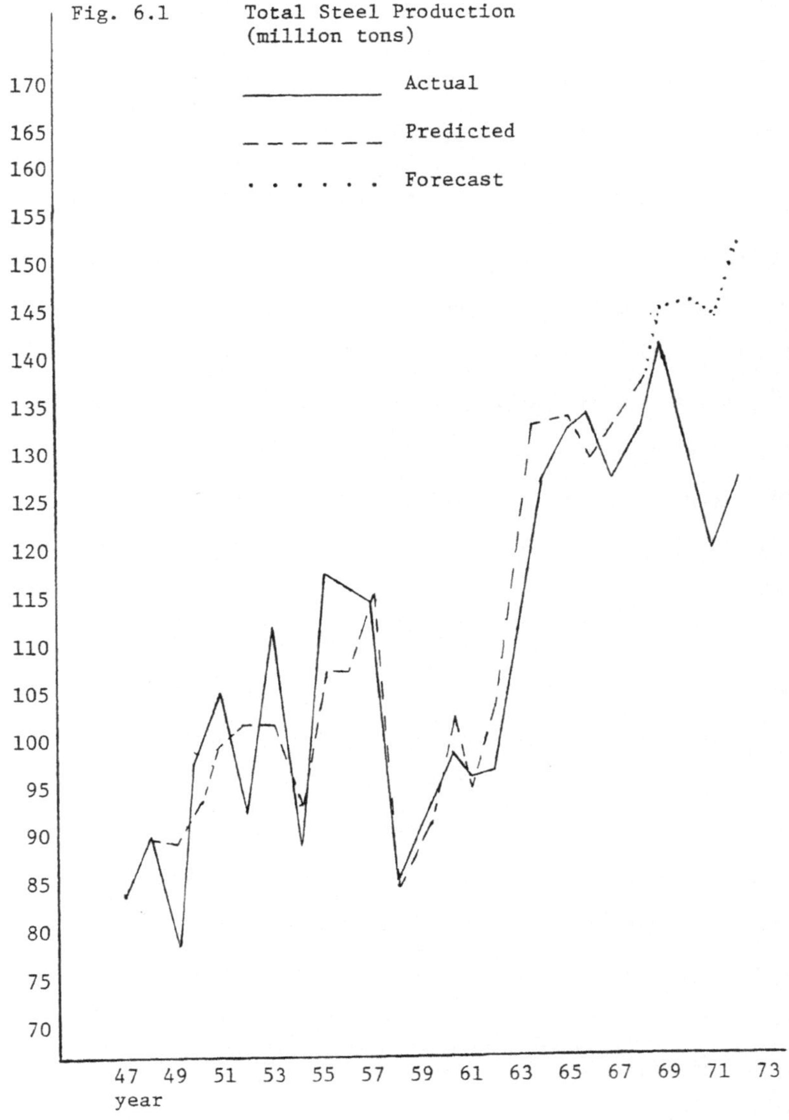
Total Steel Production
(million tons)
Actual
Predicted
Forecast
170
165
160
155
150
145
140
135
130
125
120
115
110
105
100
95
90
85
80
75
70
47 49 51 53 55 57 59 61 63 65 67 69 71 73
year

P_{IMP} - price of imported steel

P_{DOM} - price of domestically produced steel

SD_{-1} - demand for steel lagged by one period

ϵ - error term

The numbers in parenthesis are the t ratios.

The model simulated the period 1948-67 quite well (see Fig. 6.1). The fit was not good during the last three periods (1970-72) of the forecast. The regression equation was obtained from actual demand data for the period 1948-67. Using this equation, the demand was forecast for the period 1968-72 and then compared against the actual demand for that period.

This estimate could be improved by adding a dummy variable for strikes in the steel industry and a variable for the level of steel exports by other countries. Also estimating the demand for each product line separately would improve the model. Some of the over-estimation for successive years could be minimized if we had a mechanism for adjusting output taking into account inventories carried over from the previous period. This would also reduce over estimation of materials and energy required for steel production.

The demand for steel data was obtained from the AISI Annual Statistical Reports.

In the steel sector we only considered technological change in steel making. There have been innovations in the rolling and coke processes but adequate data were not available. There are four sets technological change equations one for each of the steel making technologies, Bessemer, open hearth (O.H.), electric furnace (E.F.), basic oxygen furnace (B.O.F.). It would have been desirable to estimate the equations simultaneously. Since the basic oxygen furnace was not introduced into this country until 1955, we were unable to obtain satisfactory results from a simultaneous estimation. We were forced to estimate the equations for each technology separately. This problem is discussed further when the B.O.F. equations are examined.

The four regions for the steel sector are:

Region I - N.Y.
Region II - Pa., Ohio, Michigan
Region III - Ill., Ind., Ala., Texas
Region IV - Colo. Utah, Ca.

The regions were chosen in order to be able to use Nelson's data for 1947-67 which was given by steel producing center and the AISI data for 1968-72 which was given by state.

For Nelson the Pittsburgh, Pa. - Youngstown, Ohio area represented one producing area and the Cleveland, Ohio - Detroit, Mich. region another producing center. Thus it was not possible to separate Pa., Ohio, and Michigan since some of the data we used was derived from Nelson's data. We decided to place Indiana and Illinois in the same region as Alabama and Texas primarily to equalize the output of the regions somewhat. Region II was still by far the largest steel producing section of the country.

Since there were four regions and a times series of twenty years, we pooled the data in order to obtain the estimates for the capacities of the steel making technologies for each region. For the open hearth technology we found that Regions I and IV had the same intercepts and slopes. The open hearth equations had different intercepts and different slopes for the time trend for regions II and III. The equations for the open hearth are:

Regions I and IV

$$\frac{(KOH)_i}{K_{-1}} = \underset{(9.9)}{1.14} + \underset{(1.6)}{0.017} \exp\left[40\left(\frac{REF}{ROH}\right) - 40\right] + \underset{(2.1)}{0.000018} \exp\left[5\left(\frac{RBOF}{ROH}\right) - 5\right]$$

$$- \underset{(-3.5)}{0.56} \exp\left[\frac{REF}{ROH}\right]^2 - \underset{(-4.2)}{0.06} \exp\left[\frac{RBOF}{ROH}\right]^2 - \underset{(-8.1)}{0.000036}\ IMP + \epsilon_i$$

Region II

$$\frac{(KOH)_{II}}{K_{-1}} = \underset{(9.9)}{1.14} + \underset{(54.7)}{5.81}\ D_2 + \underset{(1.6)}{0.017} \exp\left[40\left(\frac{REF}{ROH}\right) - 40\right]$$

$$+ \underset{(2.06)}{0.000018}\left[\exp 5\left(\frac{RBOF}{ROH}\right) - 5\right] - \underset{(-3.5)}{0.56} \exp\left[\frac{REF}{ROH}\right]^2 - \underset{(-4.2)}{0.06} \exp\left[\frac{RBOF}{ROH}\right]^2$$

$$- \underset{(-8.1)}{0.00036}\ IMP - \underset{(-18.0)}{0.13}\ T_2 + \epsilon_2$$

Region III

$$\frac{(KOH)_{III}}{K_{-1}} = \underset{(10.0)}{1.14} + \underset{(21.8)}{2.18}\, D_3 + \underset{(1.6)}{0.017} \exp\left[40\left(\frac{REF}{ROH}\right) - 40\right]$$

$$+ 0.000018 \exp\left[5\left(\frac{RBOF}{ROH}\right) - 5\right] - \underset{(-3.5)}{0.56} \exp\left[\frac{REF}{ROH}\right]^2$$

$$- \underset{(-4.2)}{0.06} \exp\left[\frac{RBOF}{ROH}\right]^2 - \underset{(-8.1)}{0.00036}\, IMP - \underset{(-4.5)}{0.03}T_3 + \epsilon_3$$

$(KOH)_i$ - open hearth capacity in region i

K_{-1} - total capacity lagged one period

ROH - total cost of producing one ton of steel with the open hearth furnace

REF - total cost of producing one ton of steel with the electric furnace

RBOF - total cost of producing one ton of steel with the basic oxygen furnace

IMP - tons of steel imported

D_i - dummy variable for intercept, 1 if region i, 0 otherwise

ϵ_i - error term for region i

The numbers in the parentheses are the t rations. The F statistic is 869. The R^2 is 0.98. The high R^2 arose from the use of fewer restrictions on the intercept and the slope of the regression equation. Dummy variables were introduced into the model in order to "explain" the differences in the intercepts and slopes for each

Fig. 6.2

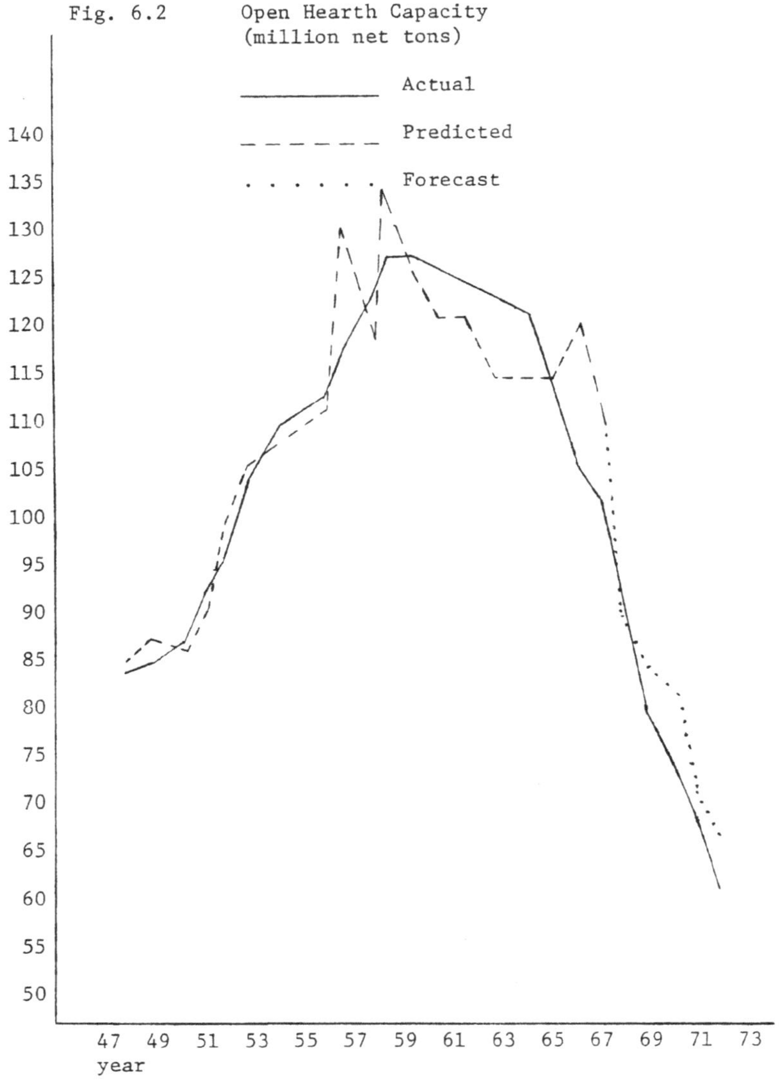
Open Hearth Capacity
(million net tons)
Actual
Predicted
Forecast
140
135
130
125
120
115
110
105
100
95
90
85
80
75
70
65
60
55
50
47 49 51 53 55 57 59 61 63 65 67 69 71 73
year

region. Thus more of the variance in the dependent variable was explained than if the usual restrictions on the slope and intercept were maintained [3; 205]. The Durbin-Watson Statistic was 2.04 which indicates that there was no positive autocorrelation.

While the relative costs of the basic oxygen furnace and the electric furnace were significant explanatory variables for all the technologies, except the Bessemer, the relative cost of the Bessemer was not significant because it was in the process of being phased out mostly due to the large amounts of pollutants emitted from the furnace relative to other technologies.

The model simulated the period 1947-67 quite well. It understated the actual data during the period when the open hearth was initially being phased out. This was probably due to the exclusion of vintage as an explanatory variable, because it was not available. The forecast for the period 1968-72 was very good. It tended to be on the high side (see Fig. 6.2). Our simulation of open hearth capacity was superior to Nelson's simulation.

The Bessemer converter was only found in Regions II and III. The data were pooled for the two regions. The equations are:

Region II

$$(KBES)_{II} = \underset{(1.9)}{1613.8} + \underset{(16.7)}{3119.5}D_2 - \underset{(-1.5)}{0.21} \exp\left[-30\left(\frac{REF}{ROH}\right) + 30\right]$$

$$+ \underset{(2.5)}{6.42} \exp 2\left[\frac{RBOF}{ROH}\right] + \underset{(1.8)}{98.6} \exp\left[-30 \frac{RBES}{ROH} + 30\right]$$

$$- \underset{(-1.9)}{0.14}\ PROD_{-1} + \epsilon_2$$

Region III

$$(KBES)_{III} = \underset{(1.9)}{1613.8} - \underset{(-1.5)}{0.21} \exp\left[-30\left(\frac{REF}{ROH}\right) + 30\right] + \underset{(2.5)}{6.42} \exp^2\left[\frac{RBOF}{ROH}\right]$$

$$+ 98.6 \exp\left[-30\left(\frac{RBES}{ROH}\right) + 30\right] - \underset{(-1.9)}{0.14} PROD_{-1} + \epsilon_3$$

$(KBES)_i$ - Bessemer capacity in region i

D_i - dummy variable, 1 region i, 0 otherwise

ROH - cost of producing steel with O.H.

RBES - cost of producing steel with Bessemer

RBOF - cost of producing steel with B.O.F.

REF - cost of producing steel with E.F.

$PROD_{-1}$ - total steel production lagged one period.

The F Statistic is 62 and the R is 0.91. The Durbin-Watson Statistic is 2.67 which indicates that there was no positive autocorrelation. The negative coefficient for PROD can be explained by the fact that if steel production is rising, then the steel industry would find it easier to replace obsolete capacity more readily than if production were stagnant. However this might not be true if production were expanding so rapidly that capacity bottlenecks occurred and obsolete capacity would then have to be utilized to meet the demand.

The model simulated the Bessemer very well for the period 1947-67 (see Fig. 6.3). After 1967 Bessemer capacity drops below one million annual tons and is no longer recorded separately by the AISI. It is

Fig. 6.3 Bessemer Capacity (million net tons)

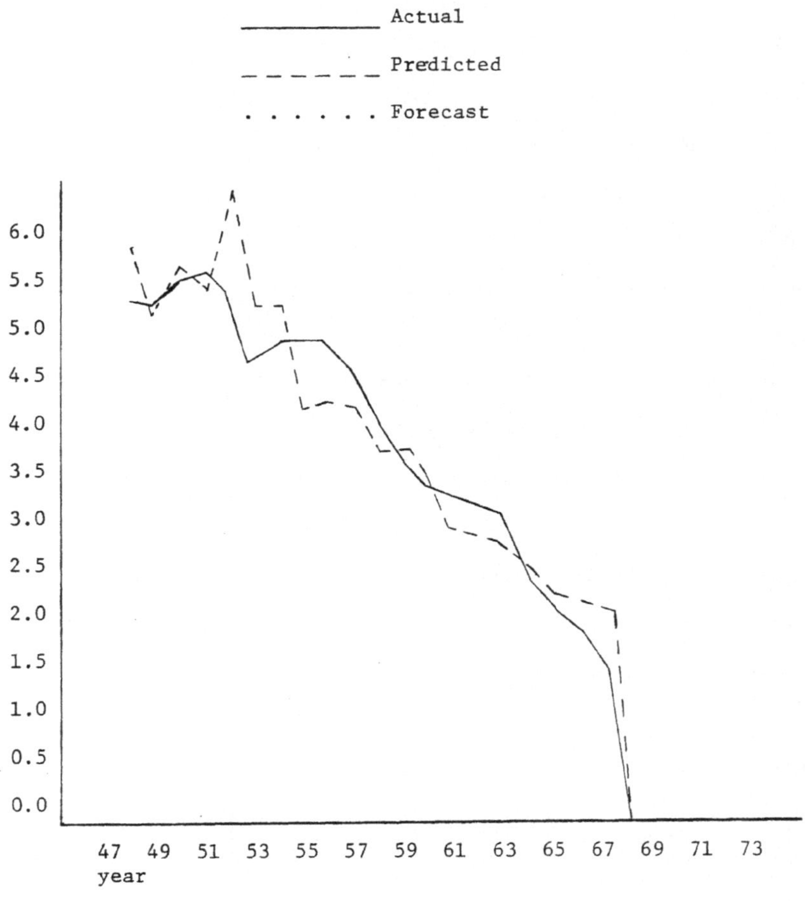

embedded in the open hearth statistics.

Many problems were encountered in our attempt to estimate basic oxygen furnace capacity since the first B.O.F. didn't go into operation until 1955. Initially we attempted to estimate the capacities of the four technologies simultaneously. Since the period we were simulating began in 1947, there was a problem in assigning a cost of production to B.O.F. before 1955. Estimates produced by Kaiser Engineers in 1954 indicated that the basic oxygen furnace would not be substantially cheaper than the open hearth ($45.79 vs. $46.40 total cost/net ton) [1; 208]. We tried using this figure, and higher cost estimates, together with additive and multiplicative dummies in order to separate pre-B.O.F. steel production. None of these attempts were successful. We were forced to simulate the capacity of each technology separately. The data was pooled for the four regions and the time series of 13 years. The equations for basic oxygen furnace capacity are:

Region I

$$\frac{(KBOF)_I}{PROD_{-1}} = \underset{(-1.8)}{-48.0} - \underset{(-2.3)}{0.75D_1} + \underset{(1.9)}{48.85} \exp\left[.01\left(\frac{REF}{ROH}\right) - .01\right]$$

$$- \underset{(-1.8)}{0.06} \exp\left[-5\left(\frac{RBOF}{ROH}\right) + 5\right] + \underset{(3.5)}{0.000033IMP} + \underset{(13.0)}{0.20T_1} + \epsilon_1$$

Fig. 6.4 Basic Oxygen Furnace Capacity (million net tons)

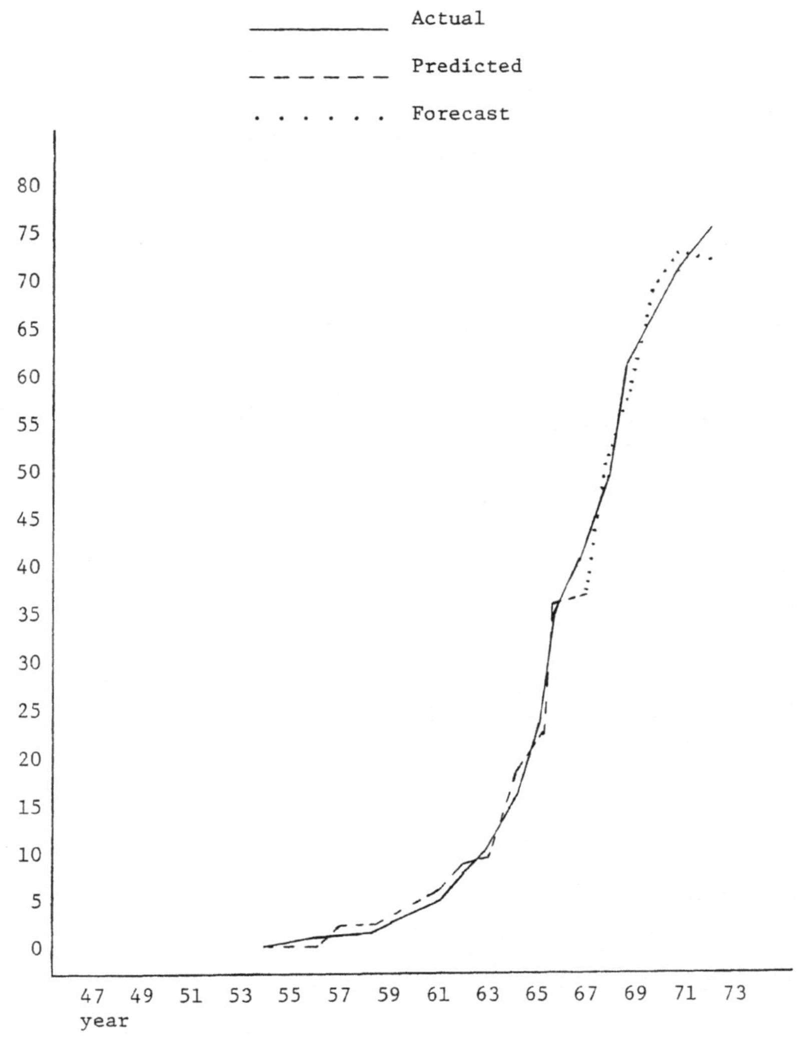

Region II

$$\frac{(KBOF)_{II}}{PROD_{-1}} = \underset{(-1.8)}{-48.0} - \underset{(-12.1)}{2.96}\, D_2 + \underset{(1.9)}{48.85} \exp\left[0.01\left(\frac{REF}{ROH}\right) - .01\right]$$

$$- \underset{(-1.8)}{0.06} \exp\left[5\left(\frac{RBOF}{ROH}\right) - 5\right] + \underset{(3.5)}{0.000033}IMP + \underset{(+2.1)}{0.05}T_2 + \epsilon_2$$

Region III

$$\frac{(KBOF)_{III}}{PROD_{-1}} = \underset{(-1.8)}{-48.0} - \underset{(-5.3)}{1.43}\, D_3 + \underset{(1.9)}{48.85} \exp\left[.01\left(\frac{REF}{ROH}\right) - .01\right]$$

$$- \underset{(-1.8)}{0.06} \exp\left[-5\,\frac{RBOF}{ROH} + 5\right] + \underset{(3.5)}{0.000033}IMP - \underset{(-2.5)}{0.04}T_3 + \epsilon_3$$

Region IV

$$\frac{(KBOF)_{IV}}{PROD_{-1}} = \underset{(-1.8)}{-48.0} + \underset{(1.9)}{48.85} \exp\left[0.01\left(\frac{REF}{ROH}\right) - .01\right]$$

$$- \underset{(-1.8)}{0.06} \exp -\left[5\left(\frac{RBOF}{ROH}\right) + 5\right] + \underset{(3.5)}{0.000033}IMP + \epsilon_4$$

$(KBOF)_i$ - B.O.F. capacity for region i

$PROD_{-1}$ - total steel production lagged one period

D_i - dummy variable, 1 if region i, 0 otherwise

T_i - time trend if region i, 0 otherwise

RBOF - cost of producing steel with B.O.F.

ROH - cost of producing steel with O.H.

REF - cost of producing steel with E.F.

IMP - tons of steel imported

The R^2 is 0.97 and the F Statistic is 181. The Durbin-Watson Statistic is 1.79 which means that there was no positive autocorrelation.

The model produced an excellent simulation of the period 1947-67 (see Fig. 6.4). The forecast also was quite good. The positive coefficient for imports indicated that the greater the imports the greater was the incentive to install the B.O.F. which was the most efficient technology.

The equations for the electric furnace capacity are:

Region I

$$\frac{(KEF)_I}{K_{-1}} = \underset{(6.4)}{0.06} - \underset{(-2.9)}{0.04}\, D_1 - \underset{(-1.5)}{0.037} \exp^{15}\left(\frac{REF}{RBOF}\right) - \underset{(-1.6)}{0.035} \exp -\left(\frac{RBOF}{ROH}\right)$$

$$+ \underset{(4.7)}{0.0011} T_1 + \epsilon_1$$

Region II

$$\frac{(KEF)_{II}}{K_{-1}} = \underset{(6.4)}{0.06} + \underset{(36.2)}{0.46}\, D_2 - \underset{(-1.5)}{0.037} \exp^{15}\left(\frac{REF}{ROH}\right) - \underset{(-1.6)}{0.035} \exp -\left(\frac{RBOF}{ROH}\right)$$

$$+ \underset{(19.2)}{0.0048} T_2 + \epsilon_2$$

fig. 6.5 Electric Furnace Capacity (million net tons)

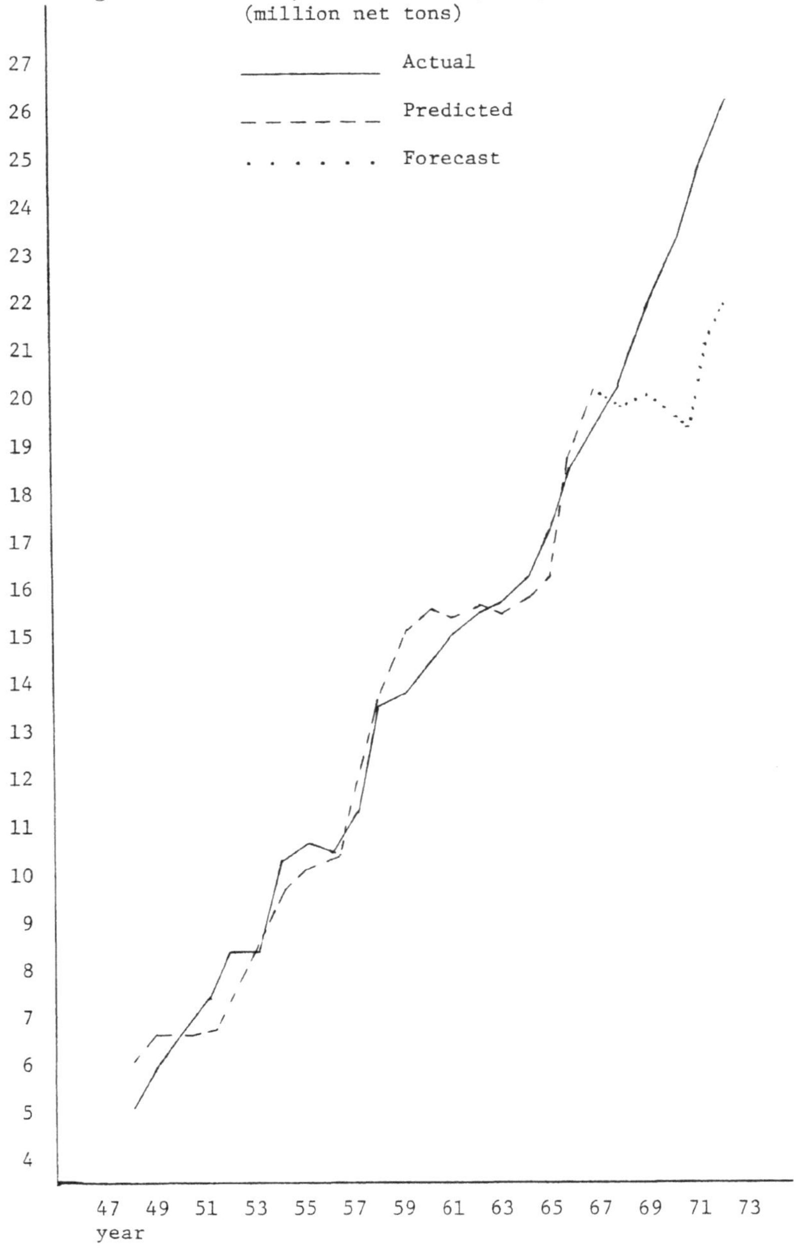

Region III

$$\frac{(KEF)_{III}}{K_{-1}} = \underset{(6.4)}{0.06} + \underset{(2.7)}{0.032D_3} - \underset{(-1.5)}{0.037} \exp^{15}\left(\frac{REF}{ROH}\right) - \underset{(-1.6)}{0.035} \exp -\left(\frac{RBOF}{ROH}\right)$$

$$+ \underset{(3.1)}{0.019T_3} + \epsilon_3$$

Region IV

$$\frac{(KEF)_{IV}}{K_{-1}} = \underset{(6.4)}{0.06} - \underset{(-1.5)}{0.037} \exp^{15}\left(\frac{REF}{ROH}\right) - \underset{(-1.6)}{0.035} \exp -\left(\frac{RBOF}{ROH}\right)$$

$$+ \underset{(1.1)}{0.0031T_4} + \epsilon_4$$

$(KEF)_i$ - electric furnace capacity for region i

K_{-1} - total capacity lagged one period

D_i - dummy variable, 1 if region i, 0 otherwise

T_i - time trend if region i, 0 otherwise

RBOF - cost of producing steel with B.O.F.

ROH - cost of producing steel with O.H.

REF - cost of producing steel with E.F.

ϵ_i - error term for region i

The R^2 is 0.99 and the F Statistic is 1221. The Durbin-Watson Statistic is 1.64 which indicates that there was no positive autocorrelation.

The model simulated the electric furnace capacity for the period 1947-67 quite well. (See Fig. 6.5). This result was improved somewhat over Nelson's simulation of the electric furnace capacity for this period. The forecast for the period 1968-72 understated the capacity. The model of electric furnace capacity might be improved by separating the E.F. capacity into those that are a part of an integrated steel operation and those that are non-integrated. An integrated steel operation would depend more on internally produced steel scrap and less on purchased scrap and thus would be less vulnerable to fluctuations in the price of scrap. An integrated operation could continue to expand and fully utilize its capacity while a non-integrated E.F. steel operation might reduce its planned expansion if continued high prices were expected. The data required to separate these two types of E.F. operations were not available.

Two important variables were excluded from our models of capacity. We attempted to include investment costs as distinct from total costs and operating cost. Serious multicollinearity problems arose when we included investment cost along with total cost or operating cost. Since total cost was considered to be a more important explanatory variable than investment cost, investment cost was not included as a variable. Since investment cost is negatively correlated with the level of investment in capacity, the model tends to understate the level of capacity. The vintage of existing capacity was also excluded as an explanatary variable since vintage data were not available. If we define vintage as the average age of existing capacity, then vintage is positively correlated with the level of investment in new capacity and negatively correlated with disinvestment in obsolete capacity. Thus the exclusion of vintage as an explanatory variable

Fig. 6.6 Scrap Steel Supply (million tons)

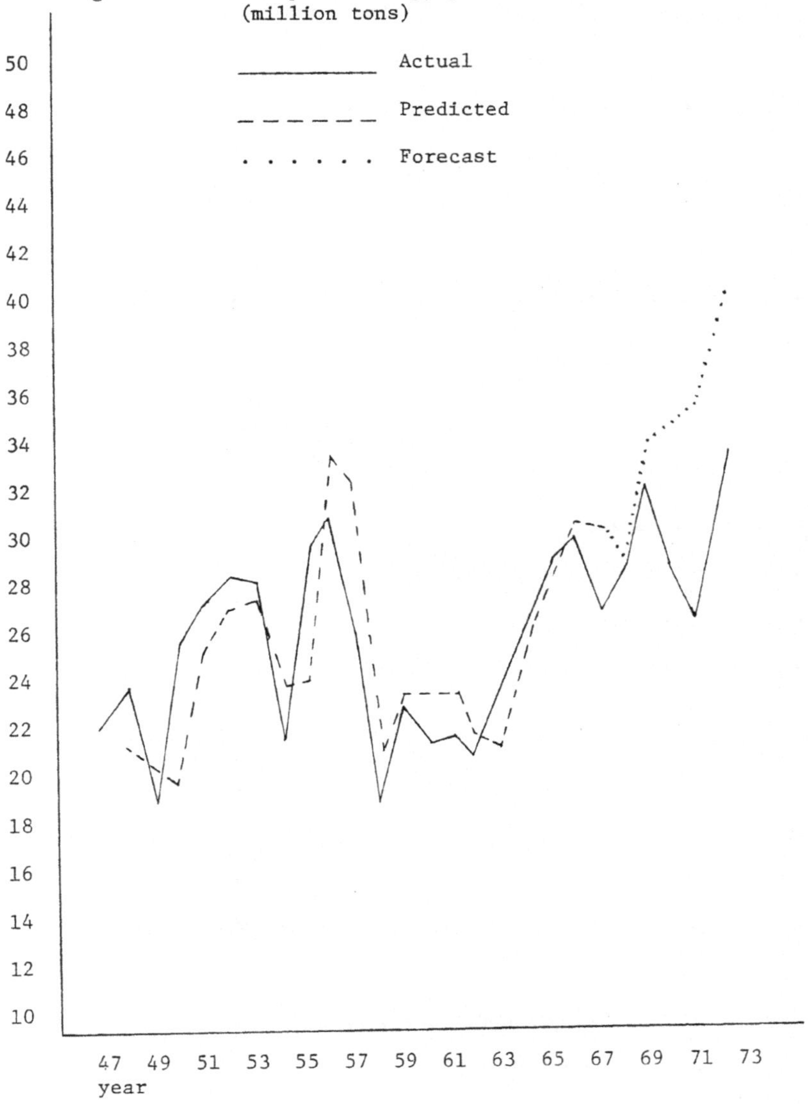

indicated that the model tended to overstate the level of capacity in B.O.F. and E.F. and understate the level of capacity in O.H.

Capacity data for 1947-60 were obtained from AISI Annual Statistical Reports and for 1961-67 from Nelson. The capacities for 1968-72 were based on a 1973 A.D. Little estimate. (See appendix for details of the derivation of capacity and cost estimates).

Scrap steel was the only input that was forecast. The equation for scrap supply is:

$$\frac{S}{M} = \underset{(-1.4)}{-0.58} + \underset{(2.4)}{0.10}\, P_s + \underset{(4.1)}{0.59}\, \frac{S_{-1}}{M_{-1}} + \epsilon$$

S - supply of scrap

M - index of manufacturing production

P_s - price of scrap

ϵ - error term

The R^2 is 0.70 and the F Statistic is 20. The Durbin-Watson Statistic is 1.43 which indicates that no conclusion can be drawn as to whether or not there is positive autocorrelation.

The model simulated the supply of scrap steel for the period 1947-67 quite well. The forecast for the period 1968-72 was not very good (see Fig. 6.6). In order to improve this model, more explanatory variables, e.g. production levels of steel fabrication, auto scrappage, etc., would be required.

The marginal cost of capital based on the cash-flow principle was computed from IRS depreciation rates and payout periods obtained by Nelson. (For details see the appendix.)

6.2.2 Static Phase

During the static phase the utilization of the steel making capacity of each of the technologies was estimated along with the amount of coal, electricity, fuel oil, natural gas, and iron ore utilized to make steel. Although we were primarily interested in the steel making process, it was necessary to examine other aspects of steel production in order to estimate the use of energy and materials in the industry as a whole if we wished to compare our estimates of the energy and materials consumption with actual consumption which is only available for the industry as a whole.

The technical coefficients we used for the four steel making technologies had the inputs from the upstream production (coke batteries and blast furnaces) incorporated into them. For example, the iron ore technical coefficients for O.H. would include the iron ore consumed in the blast furnace in order to produce the iron ingot which went into the open hearth. Thus iron ingot would no longer be an input into the open hearth. Likewise no coal is actually used in the steel refining process. However coal is used in the iron blast furnace. Thus coal becomes an input into O H. and we thereby have a technical coefficient for coal in the O.H. technology. We did not include the energy consumed in the downstream operations (rolling and finishing) in the technical coefficients. Total use of the energy inputs were adjusted to incorporate the additional energy consumed in rolling and finishing. The tables of the technical coefficients and their derivation appear in the appendix. Since there was

Fig. 6.7 Open Hearth Capacity Utilization (million net tons)

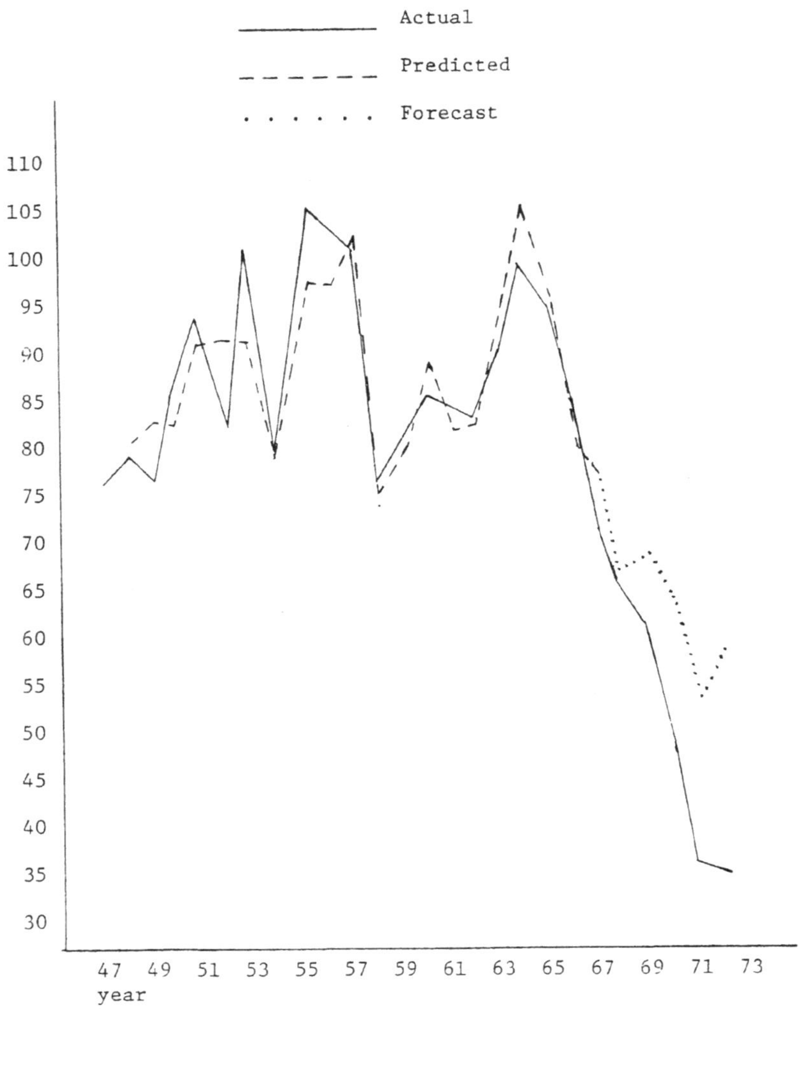

Fig. 6.8 Basic Oxygen Furnace Capacity Utilization (million net tons)

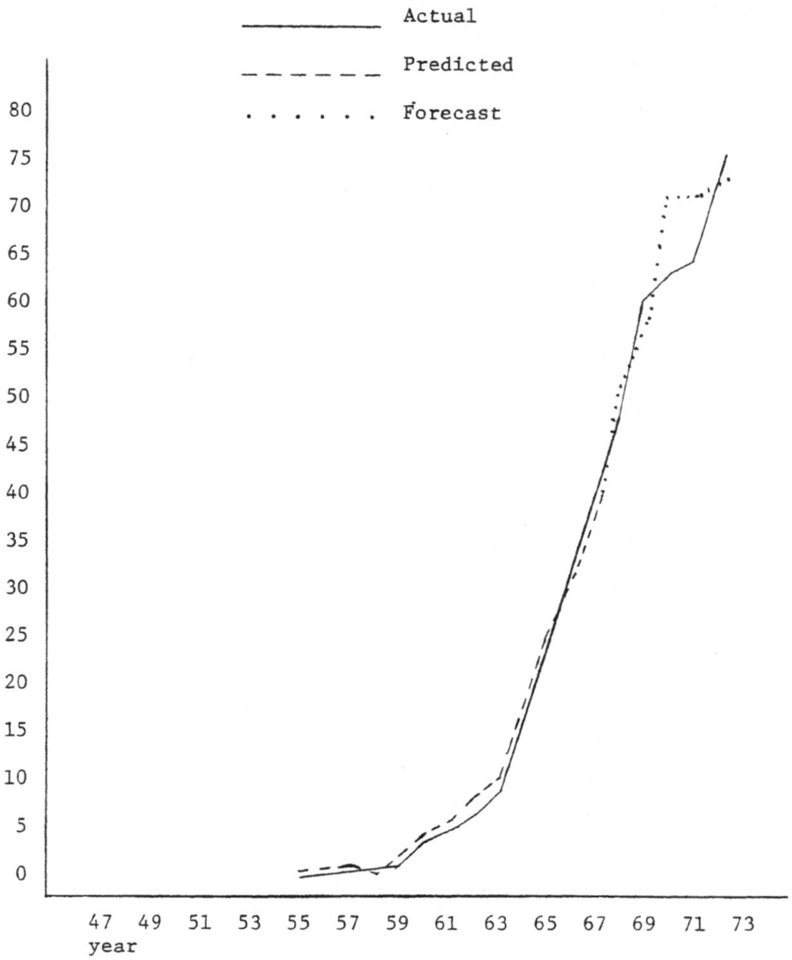

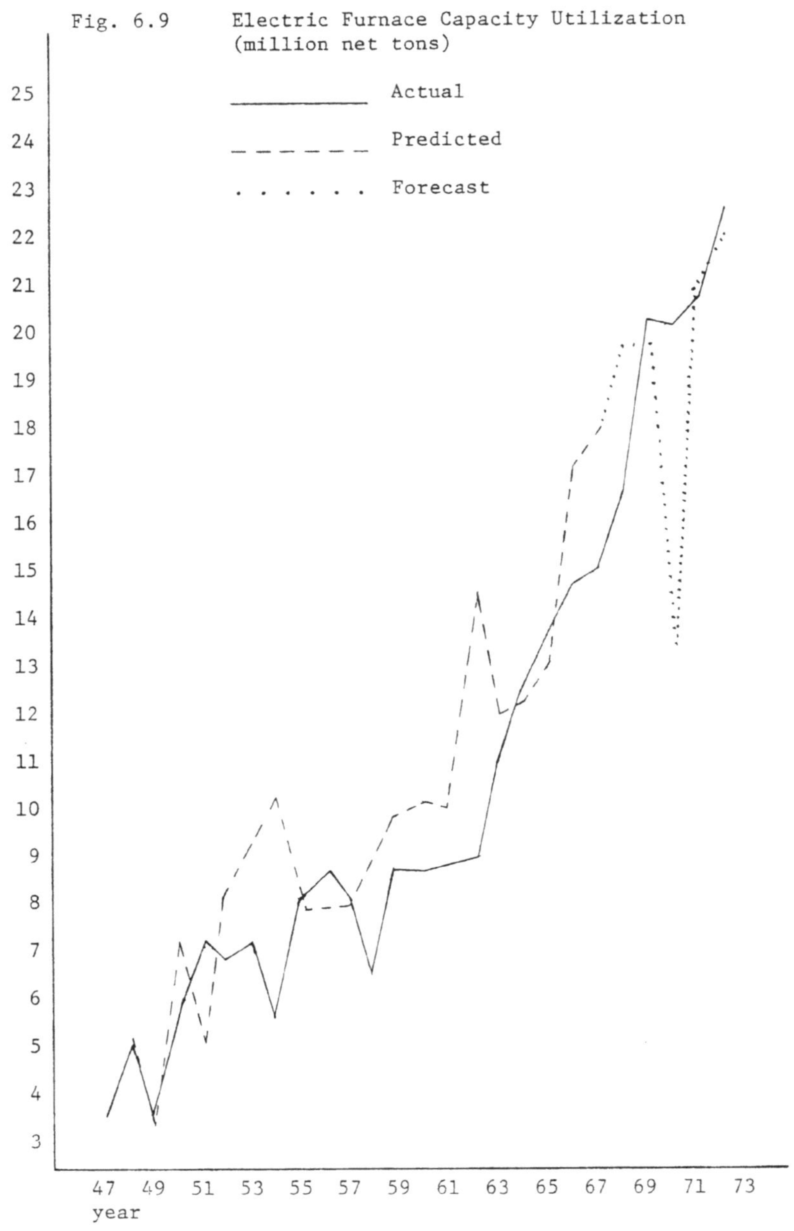
Fig. 6.9
Electric Furnace Capacity Utilization (million net tons)
Actual
Predicted
Forecast
25
24
23
22
21
20
19
18
17
16
15
14
13
12
11
10
9
8
7
6
5
4
3
47
49
51
53
55
57
59
61
63
65
67
69
71
73
year

Fig. 6.10 Bessemer Furnace Capacity Utilization (million net tons)

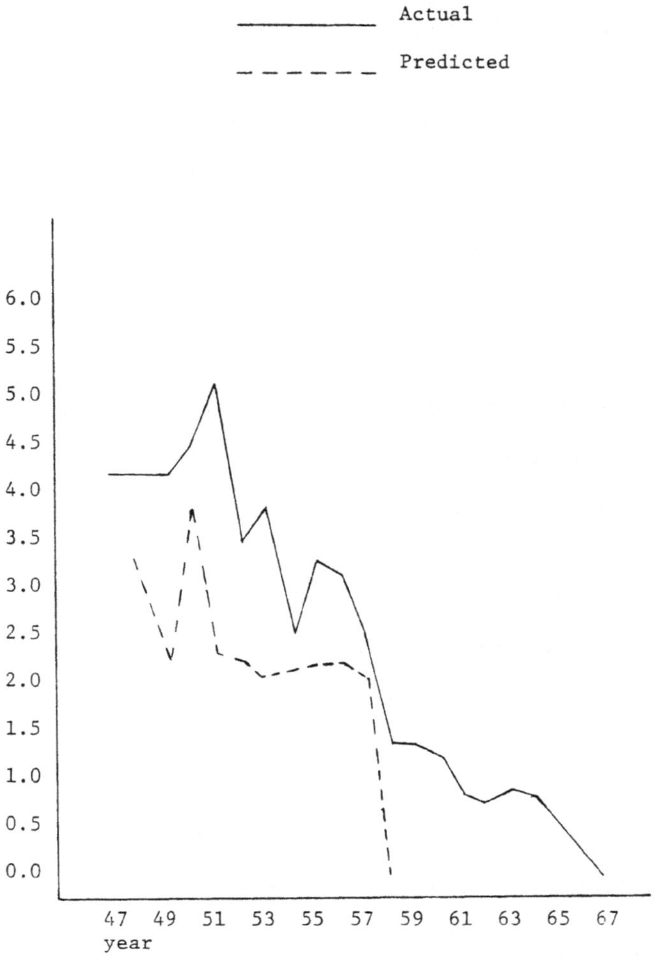

a large variability in the mix of iron input and scrap in the open hearth furnace, following Nelson, we chose three mixes, hot metal, 50/50 mix, and cold metal. Each mix had a different set of inputs. Thus, in effect we had three open hearth technologies.

The estimates of O.H. capacity utilized by the linear program for the period 1947-67 were quite good (see Fig. 6.7). The forecasts for the period 1968-72 were too high. This was due largely to the high forecast of the demand for steel. The simulation of B.O.F. capacity utilization for the period 1946-67 was excellent (see Fig. 6.8). The forecast for the period 1968-72 tended to be too high which was also due to the high forecast of the demand for steel. The simulation of electric furnace capacity utilization for the period 1947-67 tended to be too high and too sensitive to scrap prices (see Fig. 6.9). While the forecast for the period 1968-72 tended to be better than the simulation, there were still large errors for 1968 and 1970 which were due to changes in scrap prices. Using a quadratic program in place of the linear program would reduce the sensitivity of the model to fluctuations in the price of scrap. The simulation of the Bessemer utilization tended to understate it. However in terms of total steel production these errors were not large.

The simulation of the iron ore used in steel production was not bad for the period 1947-67 (see Fig. 6.11). Some of the discrepancies were due to the difficulty of fixing a technical coefficient for several years. The coefficients were held constant for the periods 1947-54, 1955-60, 1961-67, 1968-72. Also, by only allowing

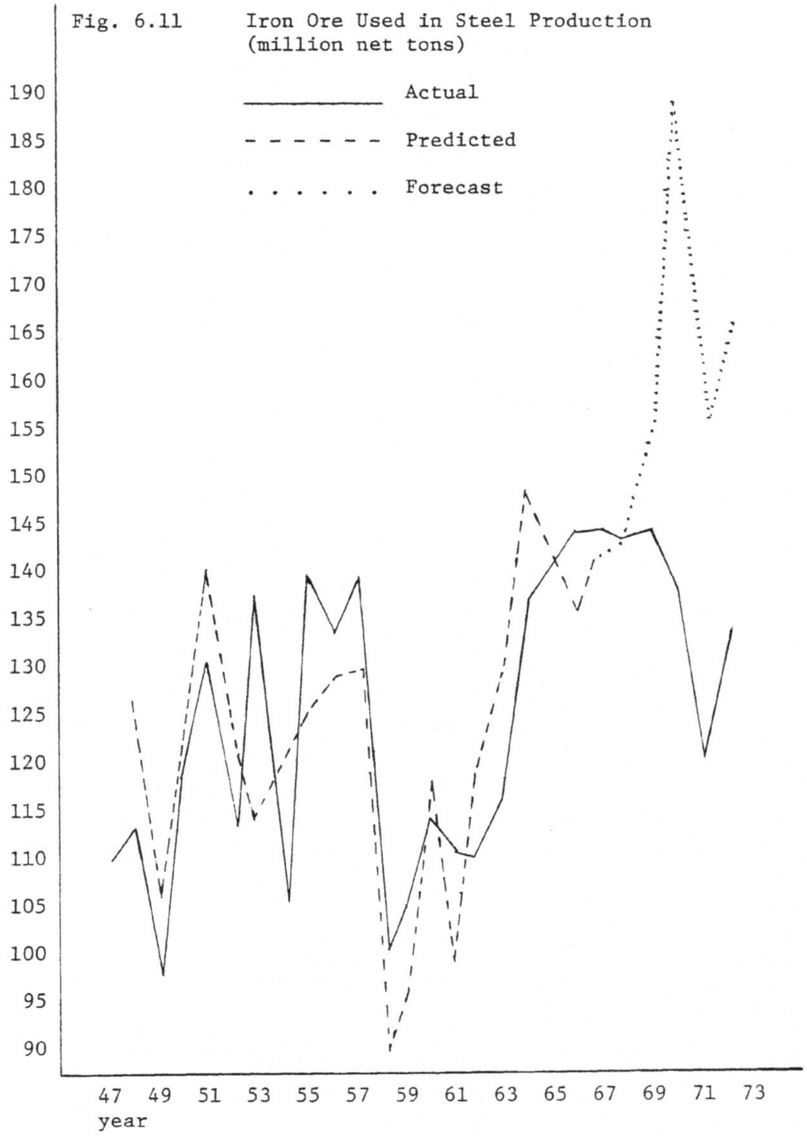
Fig. 6.11
Iron Ore Used in Steel Production
(million net tons)
Actual
Predicted
Forecast
190
185
180
175
170
165
160
155
150
145
140
135
130
125
120
115
110
105
100
95
90
47
49
51
53
55
57
59
61
63
65
67
69
71
73
year

Fig. 6.12 Coal Used in Steel Production (million net tons)

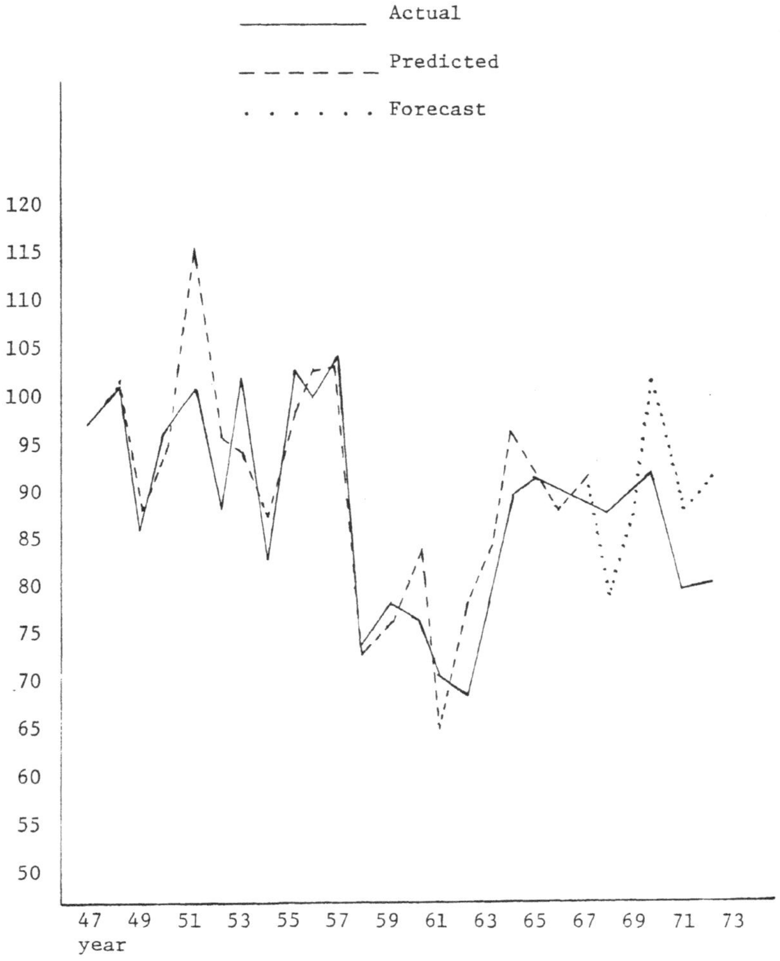

Fig. 6.13 Oil Used in Steel Production (million barrels)

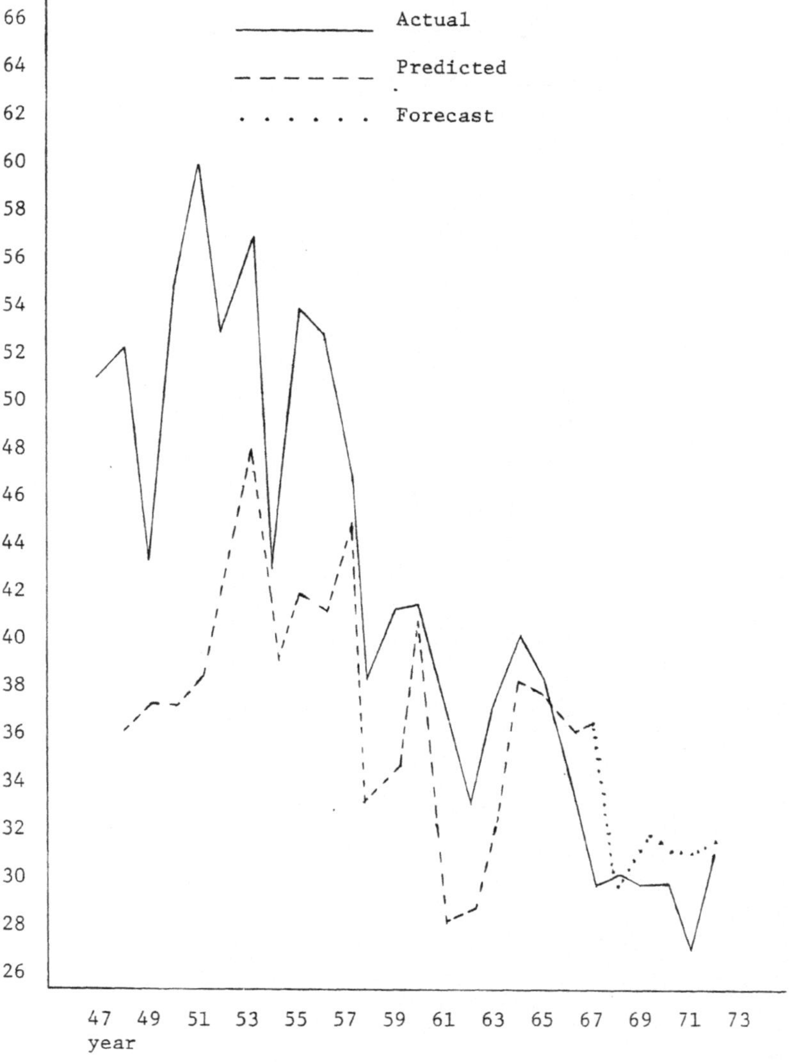

Fig. 6.14 Natural Gas Used in Steel Production (billion cu. ft.)

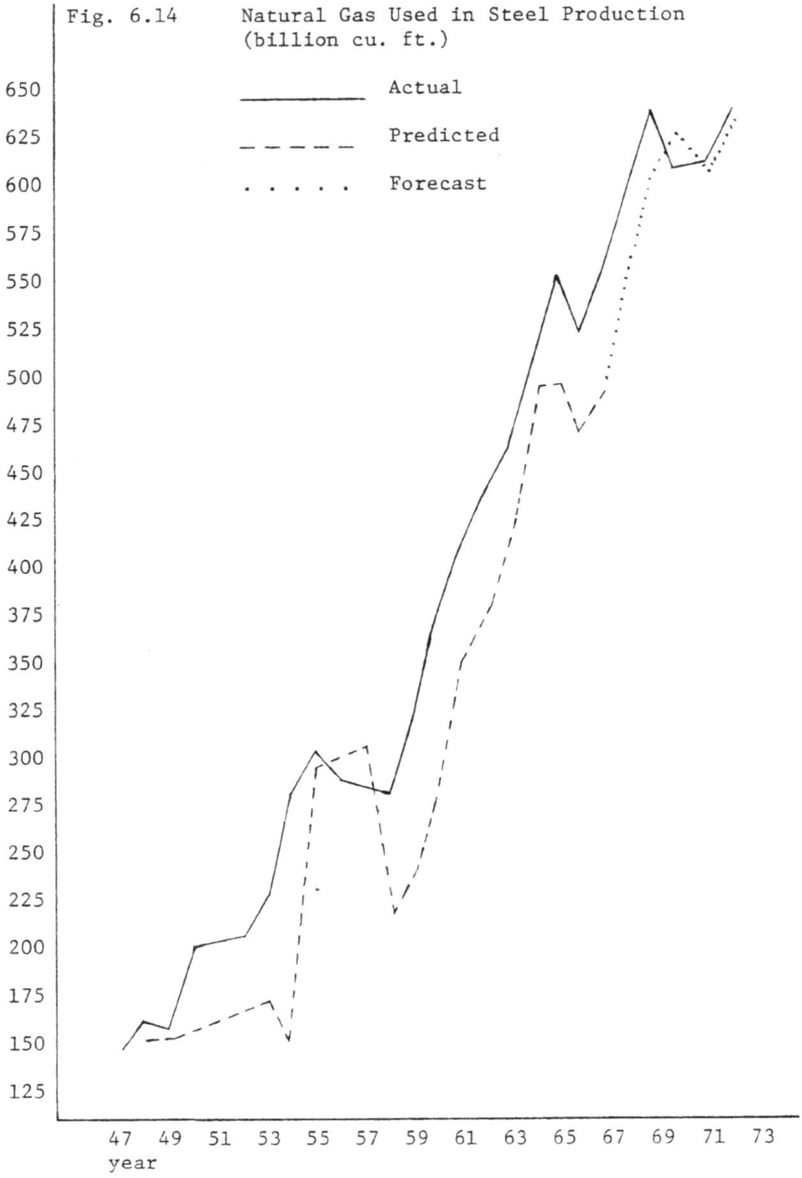

Fig. 6.15 Electricity Used in Steel Production (million kwhr)

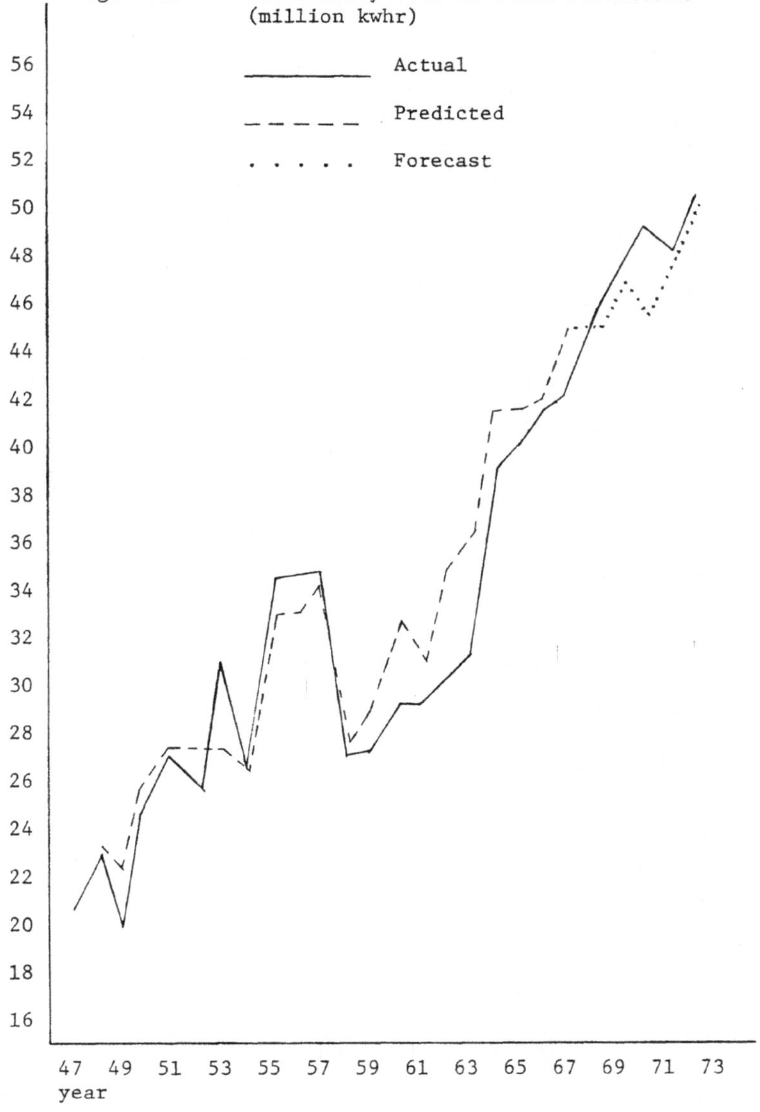

three mixes of iron ingot and scrap, the use of which depended on the prices of the materials, we introduced a certain rigidity into the open hearth technology. Also the linear program because of its linearity tends to react more to changes in prices than is actually the case. The forecast for 1968-72 was too high primarily as a result of the high forecast of the demand for steel.

The simulation of coal use in the steel industry for 1947-67 was quite good (see Fig. 6.12). The large fluctuations in the forecast for the period 1968-72 were probably due to a combination of the problem of estimating an average coal technical coefficient for that period together with the high forecast of the demand for steel.

The simulation of the fuel oil use for the period 1947-67 was poor until the sixties (see Fig. 6.13) when open hearth capacity began to be replaced with B.O.F. and E.F. The amount of fuel oil used in O.H. depended on the mix of scrap and iron ingot, the use of natural gas, and coke oven gas. The forecast tended to be too high due to the high forecast of the demand for steel.

Like fuel oil, the simulation of natural gas tended to understate natural gas consumption. Again for similar reasons (see Fig. 6.14), the forecast was much better probably due to the compensating effect of a high forecast of the demand for steel.

The consumption of electricity was dominated by its use in the electric furnace and to a lesser extent in rolling. This was seen in the simulation of electricity consumption in the steel industry which was reasonably good. The simulation tended to be too high

Fig. 6.16 Bauxite Used in Aluminum Production (million tons)

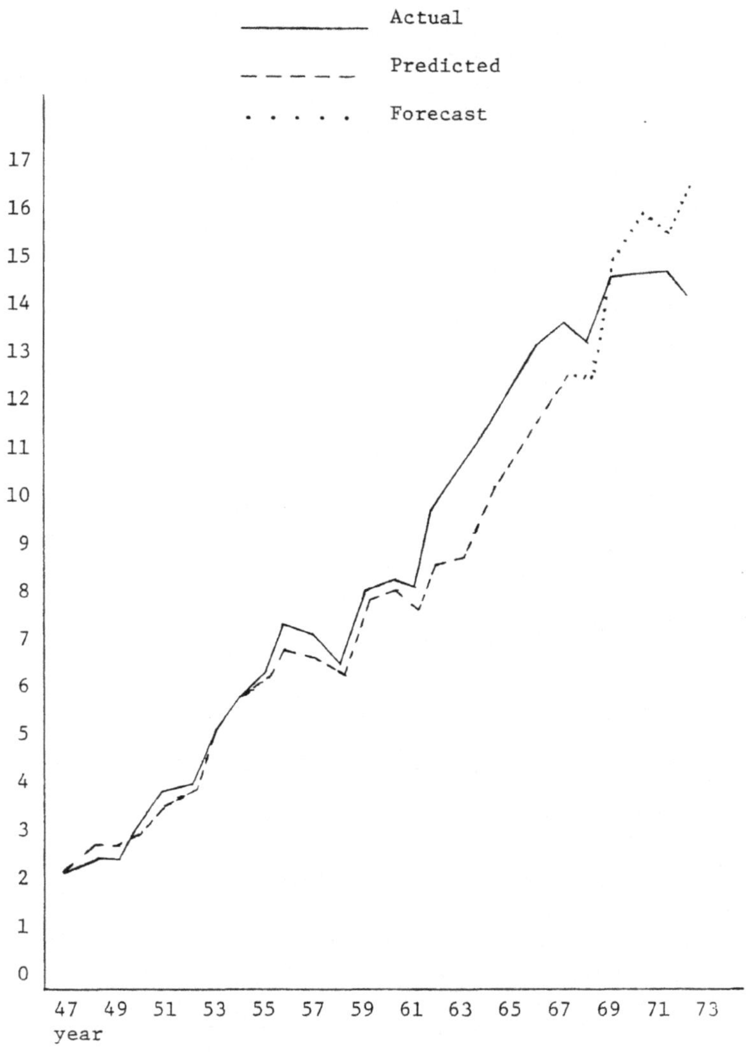

Fig. 6.17 Electricity Used in Aluminum Production (million kwhr)

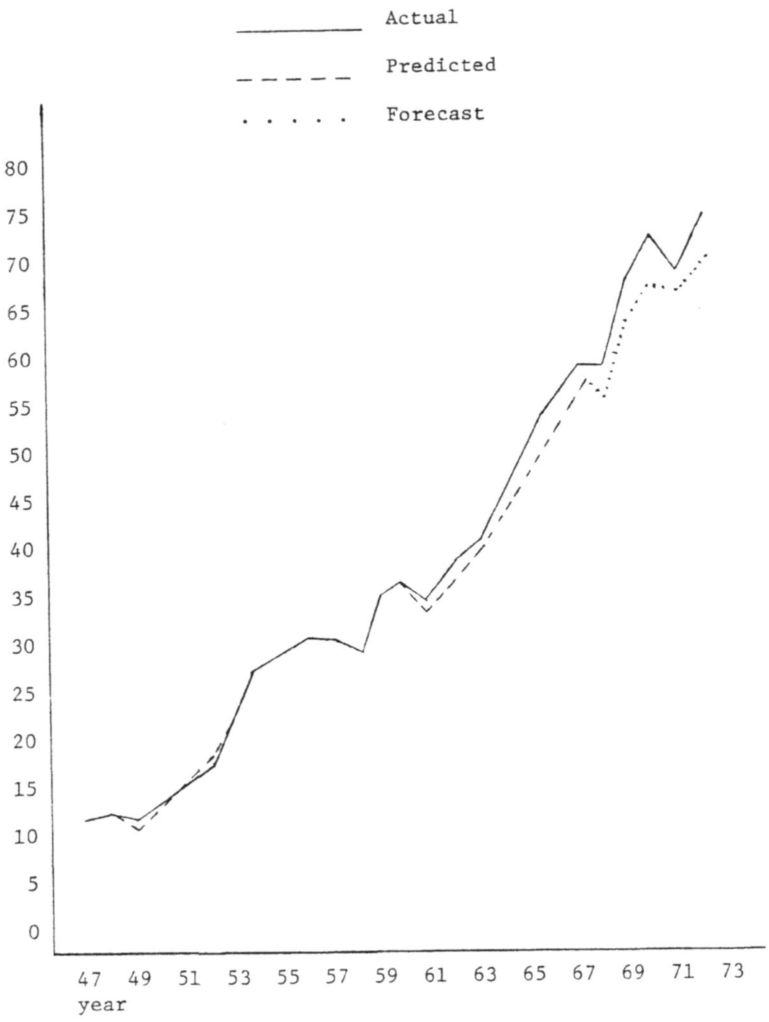

when electric furnace utilization was too high and vice-versa (see Fig. 6.15). This pattern was also evident in the forecast, notably in the dip in electricity use in 1970.

6.3 Aluminum Sector

Since there were no major innovations in aluminum production, we did not model the aluminum industry dynamically. As both capacity and production levels were also determined exogenously, we only modeled bauxite and electricity consumption in the aluminum industry.

The simulation of bauxite consumption tended to be too low during the period 1961-68 and too high from 1969-72 (see Fig. 6.16). This indicated that there were significant shifts in the grades of ore used by the aluminum industry. The simulation of electricity consumption in the aluminum industry was quite good (see Fig. 6.17). It did tend to understate electricity consumption after 1960. This could be corrected by altering the electricity technical coefficient for aluminum production.

6.4 Can Manufacturing Sector

6.4.1 Dynamic Phase

The can manufacturing industry output was divided into two products, 12 oz. beer (soda) cans which have become their most important product and the no. 2 tinplate can which was the most common size for canned fruits and vegetables. The demand for beer (soda)

Fig. 6.18 Beer Can Production
(million tons steel equivalent)

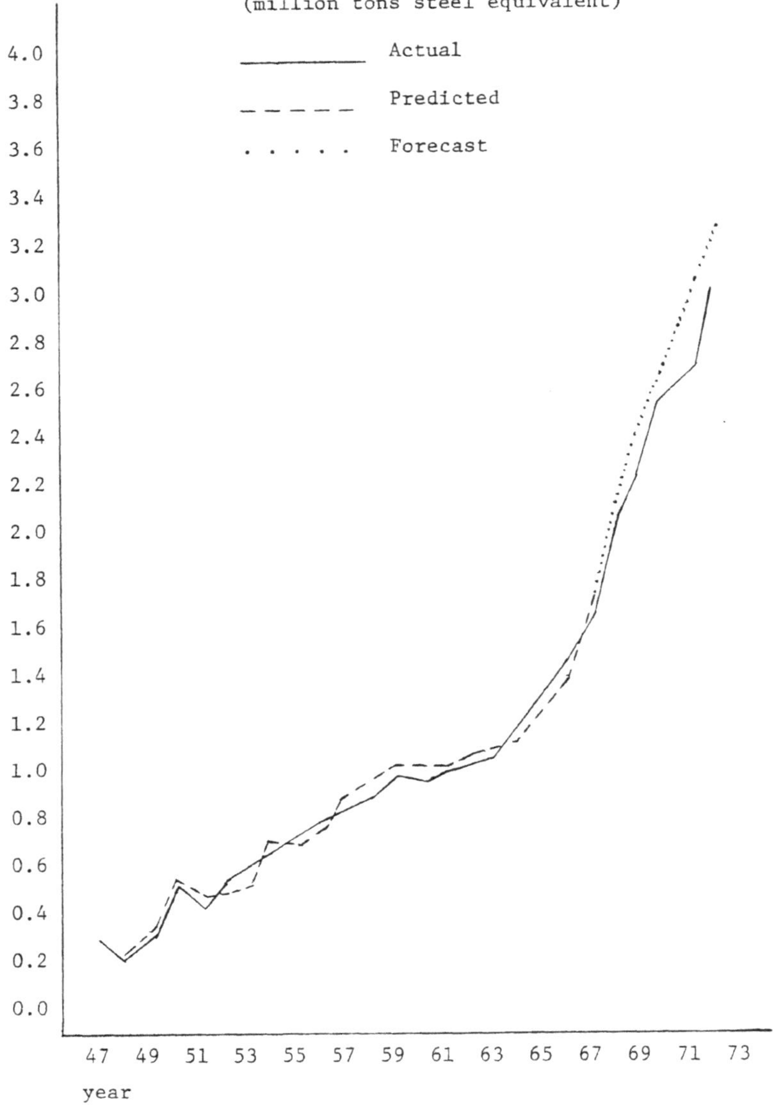

Fig. 6.19 No. 2 Tinplate Can Production (million tons)

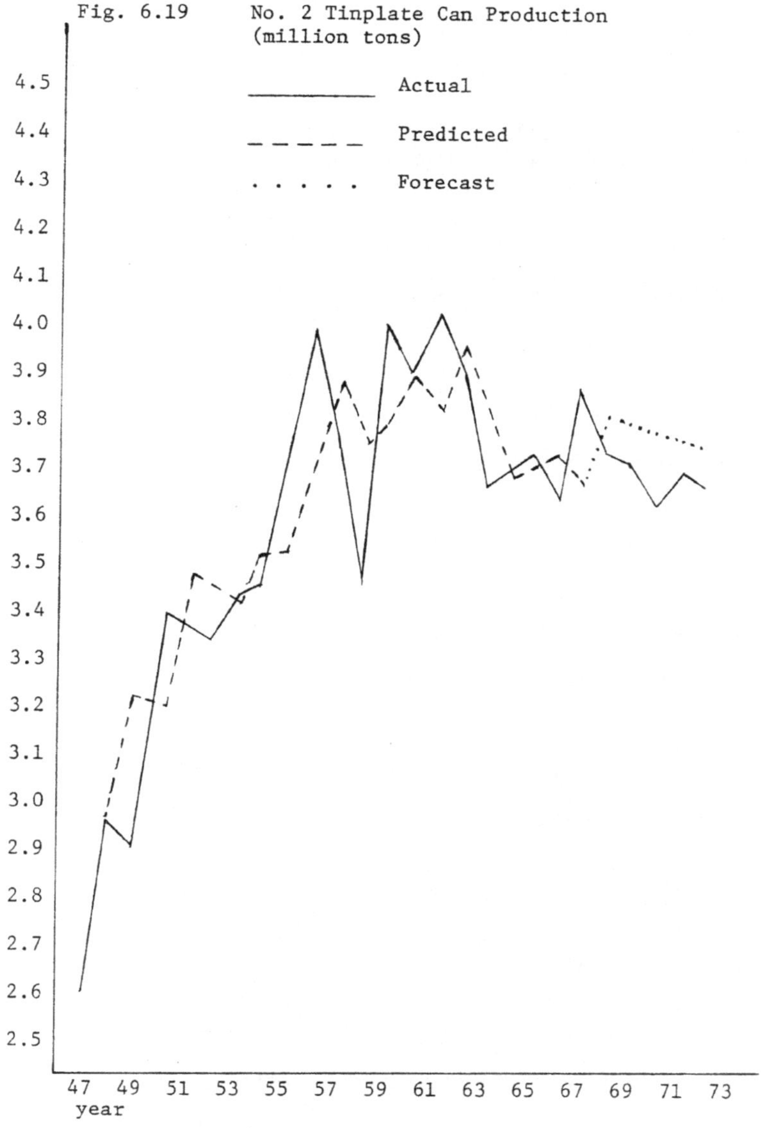

cans equation is:

$$D = \underset{(2.2)}{402.7} + \underset{(1.8)}{139.15} \frac{P_{BB}}{P_{BC}} + \underset{(21.0)}{1.21} D_{-1} + \underset{(-3.2)}{-255.02} \frac{(P_{BB})_{-1}}{(P_{BC})_{-1}} + \epsilon$$

The R^2 is 0.97 and the F Statistic is 244. The Durbin-Watson Statistic is 1.96 which indicates there was no positive autocorrelation.

D - demand for beer cans

P_{BB} - price of beer bottles

P_{BC} - price of beer cans

ϵ - error term

The simulation of the demand for beer cans was excellent. During the forecast the model did tend to over estimate beer can demand (see Fig. 6.18).

The no. 2 can was a composite product used to represent the rest of the industry. The demand for no. 2 cans has remained stable since the early fifties. The equation for the demand for no. 2 cans is:

$$D = \underset{(3.1)}{1117.3} + \underset{(7.0)}{0.7} D_{-1} + \epsilon$$

The R^2 is 0.73 and the F Statistic is 49. The Durbin-Watson Statistic is 2.41 which indicates there was no positive autocorrelation. As we can see from Fig. 6.19 the demand for no. 2 cans has remained stable since the early fifties. The simulation of the model was quite good. During the forecast period the forecast tended to be a bit on the high side.

Since the no. 2 can sector has had no major innovations, we only concerned ourselves with technological change in the beer can sector. There were two technologies for producing beer cans, the two-piece or the draw and ironed, and the three-piece. Until 1970 the two-piece can was produced exclusively with aluminum. In 1970 a few manufacturers started using a thin steelplate (coated backplate). Only since 1973 have two-piece steelplate cans been produced on a large scale. The Department of Commerce does not separate tinplate can production from steelplate can production. Until this is done, it would be impossible to take two-piece steelplace can production into account. The three-piece can was the older technology which used tinplate exclusively.

Since we only had two technologies, we only simulated three-piece beer can capacity and took two-piece can capacity to be the residual of total beer can capacity and three-piece capacity. Two-piece can production (draw and ironed) did not begin until 1963. Thus there was nothing to simulate until 1963. We started our simulation in 1963 and ran it through 1969. In order to get more data points, we estimated capacity quarterly. Our forecast period in this case went from 1970 to 1972. (See the appendix for a more detailed discussion of capacity estimates.) The equation for the three-piece beer can capacity is:

$$\frac{K3C}{R} = \underset{(12.7)}{57.14} - \underset{(-1.8)}{0.58} \exp\left[-90 \frac{R2C}{R3C} + 90\right] + \underset{(6.1)}{0.058} K_{-1} - \underset{(-4.4)}{0.019T} + \epsilon$$

Fig. 6.20 Three Piece Beer Can Capacity (million net tons annual)

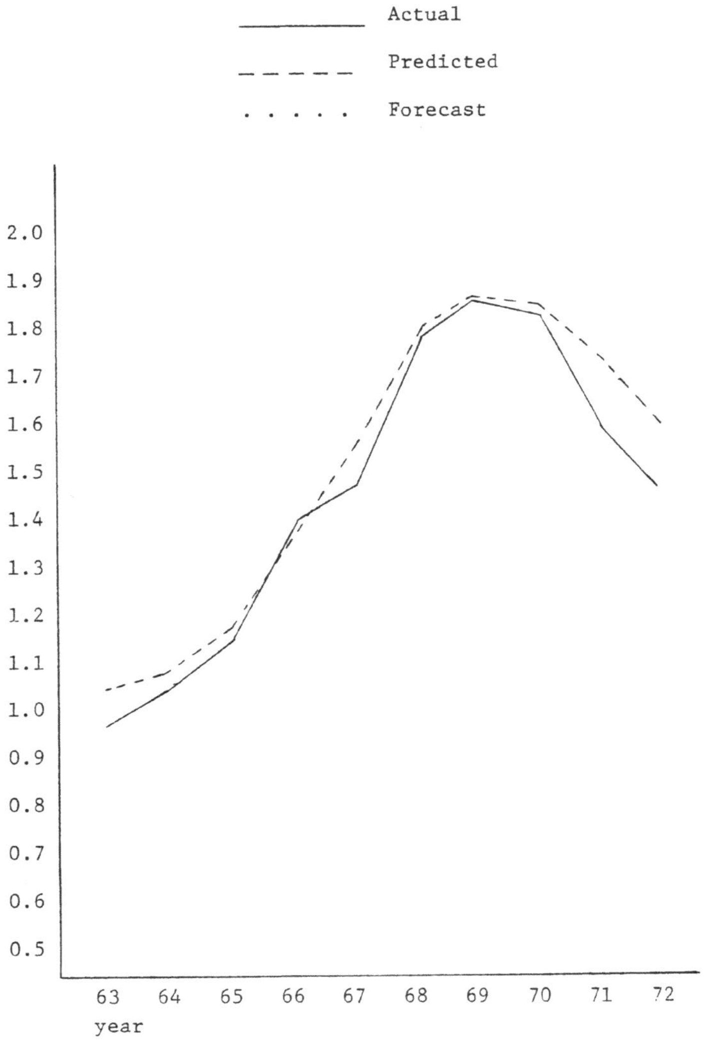

K3C - three-piece can capacity

R - interest rate

R3C - cost of production with three-piece technology

R2C - cost of production with two-piece technology

T - time trend

ϵ - error term

The R^2 is 0.72 and the F Statistic is 12.6. The Durbin-Watson Statistic is 2.36 which indicates there was no positive autocorrelation.

The simulation of the model was very good (see Fig. 6.20). During the forecast period the model tended to overstate the capacity. This was probably due to the poor quality of the data and the lack of vintage or regional data (see the appendix).

Since both the aluminum plate and tinplate were outputs of the aluminum and steel sectors, respectively, no supply equations for these inputs were needed. The marginal cost of capital, as determined by the cash-flow payoff principle, is computed in the appendix.

6.4.2 Static Phase

Since three and two piece capacity was measured in tons and since for the purposes of our model only tinplate was used in three-piece cans and aluminum in two-piece cans, the quantity of aluminum consumed in beer can production would be the same as the level of two-piece beer can production and the quantity of tinplate consumed in beer can production would be the same as the level of three-piece

Fig. 6.21 Tin Plate Used in Beer Can Production (million tons)

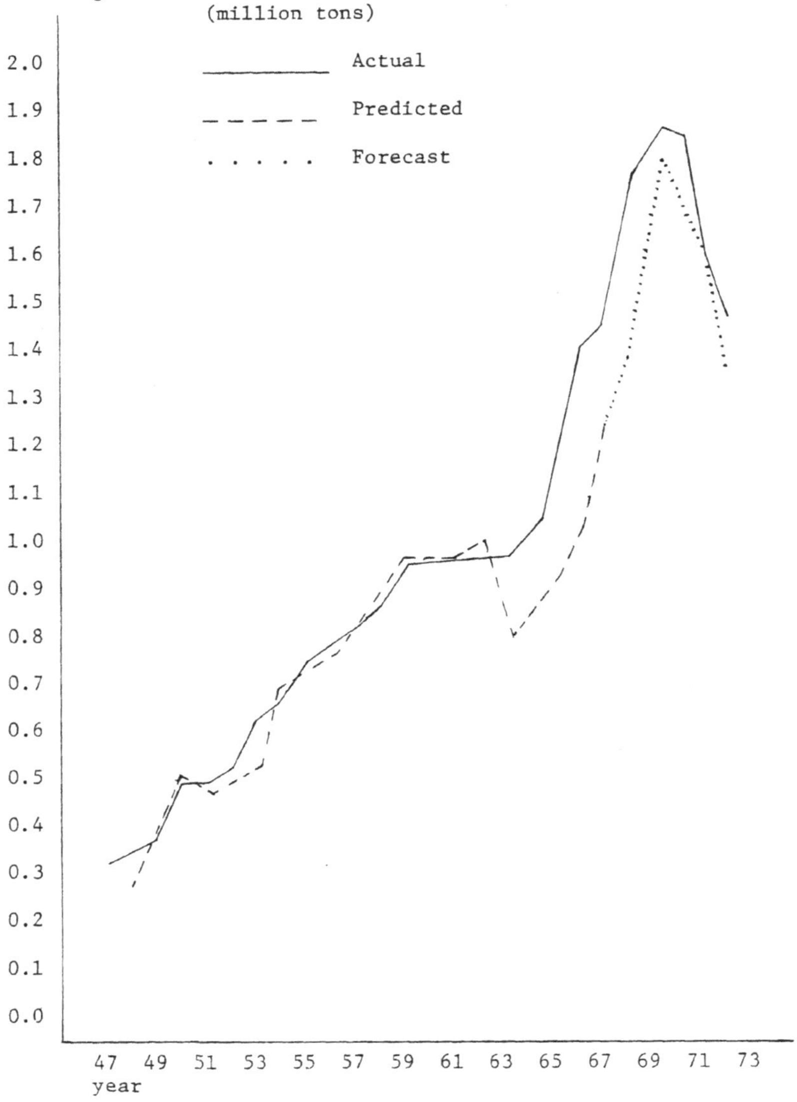

Fig. 6.22 Aluminum Used in Beer Can Production (1000 tons)

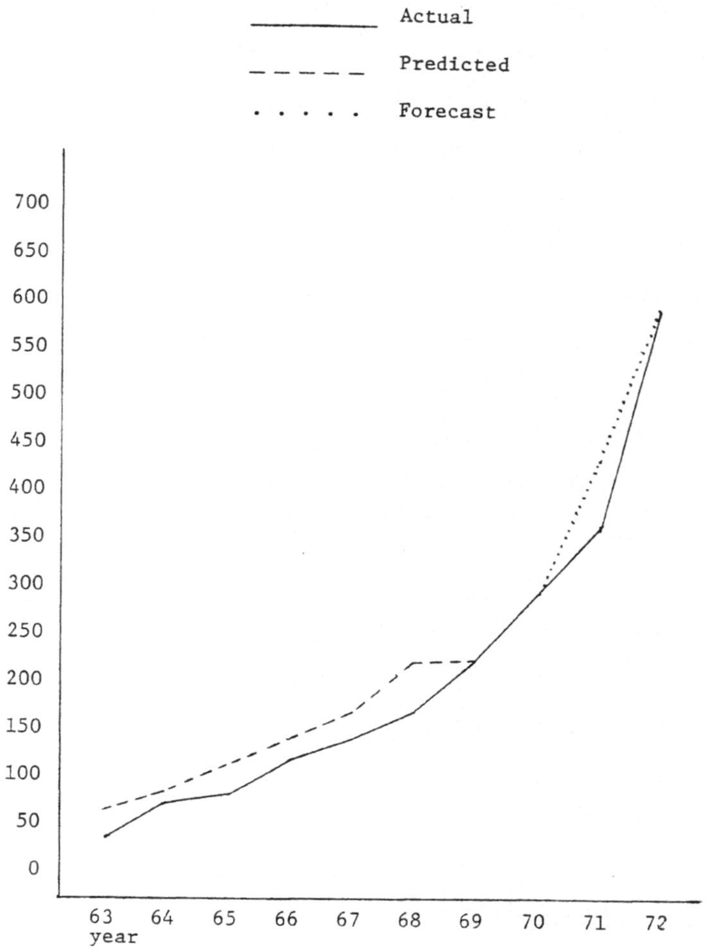

beer can production. Thus we only considered the tinplate used in beer can production and the aluminum used in beer can production.

The simulation of the model for tinplate used in beer can production was quite good (see Fig. 6.21). It understated tinplate consumption from 1963-68 and overstated aluminum consumption (see Figs. 6.21 and 6.22). This was due to the fact that the economics of two-piece technology was so far superior to three-piece technology that the only constraints were two-piece capacity and the availability of aluminum can stock. In fact, since the inception of two-piece can production, it has operated at capacity while three-piece can manufacturing lines have rapidly been dismantled and scrapped or shipped overseas. Also contributing to the understating of tinplate consumption was the difficulty of computing an average tinplate technical coefficient. The weight of a tinplate beer can has rapidly been reduced particularly in the sixties. While we had data on the lightest tinplate in use, we did not have data on the average weight of tinplate beer cans. Thus we probably underestimated the average weight of a tinplate beer can. Aside from over estimating aluminum usage in beer cans somewhat during the simulation period, the model estimated aluminum consumption in beer cans quite well particularly in the forecast period (see Fig. 6.22).

6.5 Estimating the Technical Coefficients

Now we are ready to compute the technical coefficients for the energy and materials use in the steel, aluminum, and can manufacturing sectors. The specific coefficients we will be computing are iron ore, coal, electricity, fuel oil, and natural gas use in the steel mills; bauxite and electricity use in primary aluminum; and tinplate and aluminum use in the metal cans industry. The corresponding official coefficients could not be used, in many cases, as they were given. Imports of aluminum and steel are treated as inputs to the aluminum and steel industries respectively. The imports had to be removed from the gross output of these sectors otherwise the coefficients would be distorted. There is a large input of secondary aluminum into the primary aluminum sector which also had to be removed. The 1947 and 1958 input output tables were not balanced and thus are less accurate than the 1963 and 1967 tables (see the appendix for a detailed discussion).

With the exception of the fuel oil coefficients for the steel sector, most of the estimated coefficients are quite close to the official coefficients (see Table 6.1). The 1947 iron ore coefficient for the steel sector is much higher than the official one. This is due to the over estimation of iron ore consumption by the model. The 1958 estimated coal coefficient is too low. The estimated consumption of coal in tons is very close to the actual consumption. The difference is possibly due to an error in the 1958 table or in my price estimates. The 1967 estimated electricity coefficient for the steel sector is too high. This is due to the high estimate for electric furnace utilization. Fuel oil is used in the steel industries to supplant coke oven gas and natural gas. The poor estimate of fuel oil use is due, in part, to the fact that the model does not include coke production explicitly in the model and the coke oven gas

Table 6.1

Technical Coefficients

Year / Industry	Official 1947	1958	1963	1967	Estimated 1947	1958	1963	1967	1972
Steel									
Iron Ore	.06570	.05881	.05846	.05958	.08631	.06151	.05534	.06501	.05023
Coal	.05313	.03234	.02321	.02543	.05254	.02778	.02161	.20750	.03370
Electricity	.02365	.01301	.01336	.01345	.02399	.01423	.01474	.01585	.01306
Fuel Oil	.01580	.00838	.00665	.00382	.00998	.00558	.00355	.00323	.00284
Natural Gas	.00505	.01058	.01115	.01199	.00552	.00670	.01070	.01050	.01046
Aluminum									
Bauxite	.08617	.12194	.12154	.11175	.08694	.10392	.12405	.11751	.09344
Electricity	.13608	.08192	.10686	.08761	.14700	.08565	.10067	.09103	.10370
Can Manuf.									
Tinplate	.48667	.45763	.41466	.37263	.52209	.50736	.50553	.38500	.28246
Aluminum	--	--	.01559	.04526	--	--	.02543	.04679	.08862

as an input is ignored. Natural gas, at least until recently, was the preferred choice to supplant coke oven gas since it was cheaper. The natural gas estimate for 1958 is too low as a result of the low estimate for natural gas consumption by the model.

The estimates of the bauxite and electricity coefficients for the aluminum sector are good. This is to be expected for electricity since there is only one technology to choose. Also the aluminum industry was not modeled dynamically thus reducing the possibility of errors. The 1963 tinplate and aluminum estimated coefficients for the can manufacturing industry are too high due largely to our low estimate for the value of the cans (this is a problem for all of the years and is discussed further in the appendix). Estimation of aluminum consumption is too high. Overall the coefficients are estimated quite closely. The official 1972 input output tables should be released some time during 1978. It will be interesting to see how good our forecasts will be for 1972.

References

1. Nelson, Jon P., An Interregional Recursive Programming Model of the U.S. Iron and Steel Industry: 1947-1967, University of Wisconsin, Ph.D. Dissertation, 1970.
2. Maddala, G.S., Econometrics, McGraw-Hill Co., New York, 1977.
3. Pindyck, Robert and Rubinfeld, Daniel, Econometric Models and Economic Forecasts, McGraw-Hill Co., New York, 1976.
4. Theil, Henri, Principles of Econometrics, Wiley Inc., New York, 1971.
5. The American Iron and Steel Institute, Annual Statistical Report, 1947-1973, New York.

Chapter VII

Conclusions and Extensions

7.1 Summary

The objective of this study has been to examine technological change, investment, energy and materials consumption, and production in three sectors of the economy; steel, aluminum, and can manufacturing. In the steel sector we just examined technological change in the steel making process. We modeled the period 1947-1967 and forecast the above for the period 1968-72. A dynamic model was developed for this purpose. The model consisted of a static phase, which was a linear program, and a dynamic phase, which was an econometric submodel. During the static phase the level of utilization of the capacity of each of the steel making technolgies was decided based on the cost of utilizing the various technologies. This in turn determined the consumption of the materials and energy required for the production of steel. We assumed that no investment decision would be made during the static phase since it was assumed that investment decisions would be based on long run considerations rather than short run factors. The static phase had a duration of one year.

Investment decisions were made during the dynamic phase. The level of investment or disinvestment in the three competing steel making technologies, the open hearth, the electric furnace, and the basic oxygen furnace, were estimated by the technological change equation. This was the major difference between this model and the earlier recursive programming models of Day and Nelson. In Day's and Nelson's models, investment decisions are made during the static phase.

Lastly we attempted to estimate the technical coefficients for the years 1947, 1958, 1963 and 1967 for the iron ore and energy inputs into the steel sector, bauxite and electricity inputs into the aluminum sector, and aluminum and steel inputs into the metal can sector.

7.2 Conclusions

Our original intention in considering the steel, aluminum, and can manufacturing sectors was to examine the interaction of the three sectors as the aluminum and steel industries competed for the metal can market. However it turned out that this competition did not begin until 1971 and therefore was too recent for us to model this behavior. Also no new aluminum reduction technologies became commercial during the period 1947-1972. If the new chlorine process is shown to be commercially viable, then it would be interesting to see how well the model would estimate the rate of adoption of this new technology.

While our results for the steel industry are an improvement over the earlier work of Nelson, they still leave something to be desired. Some of the causes of the less than desirable results were due to the exclusion of two important variables from the technological change equations. Investment cost, as distinct from total and operating cost, was excluded as an explanatory variable for the technological change equation as a result of multicollinearity problems. The vintage of the capacity for each of the technologies could not be included as a variable due to the lack of vintage data. A more sophisticated model for forecasting the demand for the output of the industry might have produced better forecasts of the energy and materials consumption, and the level of the capacity of the various technologies for the forecast period. The poor quality of the available data and the lack of regional data made it very difficult to model the can manufacturing industry.

With the exception of the fuel oil coefficients for the steel sector, most of the estimated coefficients for that sector were reasonable. The estimates of the technical coefficients for the aluminum sector were generally good. The estimates of the coefficients for the metal can industry were not good which tends to reflect the poor quality of the data for that industry.

7.3 Extensions

There are other approaches that one can take which may improve the model. Developing a more sophisticated model for estimating the future demand for the output of the industry might improve the forecasts derived from the model.

One of the problems we encountered was our inability to estimate the technological change equations for the steel industry simultaneously, since the basic oxygen furnace technology was not introduced until 1954. Thus we were unable to use all of the available information in estimating the technological change equations. The estimates would be improved if it were possible to estimate the equations simultaneously.

If one were to use the conditional logit analysis developed by McFadden, this problem would not arise. This is a technique that has been developed for model specification and estimation of decision making processes where the decision maker is faced with several discrete choices. The use of this technique might also make it possible to use investment costs and total costs as explanatory variables. Joskow and Mishkin have successfully used the conditional logit analysis to study electricity fuel choice behavior [2]. Since choice of fuel in electric power generation essentially amounts to a choice of technology, where the decision maker is considering new investments in generating capacity, the problem they face is similar to the one we faced. Thus it would appear that the use of the conditional logit analysis would improve our model.

References

1. Fuss, Melvyn and McFadden, Flexibility Versus Efficiency in Ex Ante Plant Design, Discussion Paper No. 190, Harvard Institute of Economic Research, Harvard University, Cambridge, Mass., 1971.

2. Joskow, Paul and Mishkin, Frederic, Electric Utility Fuel Choice Behavior in the United States, Unpublished, 1974.

APPENDICES

Appendix A

Steel Industry

Much of the data for the steel industry was obtained from Nelson and the AISI Annual Statistical Reports. The prices of imported steel for the period 1947-65 were obtained from Higgens, Christopher, "An Econometric Description of the U.S. Steel Industry", Ed. Lawrence R. Klein, Studies in Quantitative Economics No. 4., University of Pennsylvania, Philadelphia, 1969. The price of imported steel for the period 1966-72 was obtained from the Statistical Abstract of the U.S. Higgens has produced a time series of weighted average prices for imported steel products which he obtained from unpublished sources. The Statistical Abstract only gives the average price for imported steel tubes and pipes from 1960 on a regular basis. In order to extend Higgens' time series to 1972 we used 1965 as a reference year. Then we took the ratio of Higgens' price to the Statistical Abstract price. Using this ratio and the Statistical Abstract price we obtained the estimated prices from 1966-72 that were compatible with Higgens' time series.

The indices of manufacturing production were obtained from the Statistical Abstract. The cost of producing steel with each technology was obtained from the technical coefficients for each technology, the prices for the inputs, and the depreciation of the equipment. (For a more detailed discussion of the components of the cost see below.) Quantity of imports data were obtained from the AISI

Table A.1

Steel Capacity Estimates

(Million NT/yr)

Year	Nelson	Bosworth	ECE	A.D. Little	Levinson
1961	147.7	149.8	148.8		
1962	149.3	150.4	149.4		
1963	150.9	151.1	151.0		
1964	154.9	151.9	153.8		
1965	156.1	152.7	156.5		
1966	160.2	153.5			
1967	161.8	154.2			
1968		155.0			162.0
1969		155.5			162.2
1970		155.5			162.4
1971		156.2			162.6
1972		154.6			162.8
1973		155.0		163.0	163.0

Table A.2

Capacity Estimates by Technology
(Thousands NT/yr)

Year	O.H.	E.F.	B.O.F.
		Levinson	
1968	91,492	20,695	49,813
1969	79,077	21,937	61,236
1970	72,818	23,253	66,429
1971	67,858	24,648	70,244
1972	60,289	26,127	76,584
		A.D. Little	
1973	49,000	28,000	86,000

Annual Statistical Reports. Capacity data for 1947-60 were obtained from AISI Annual Statistical Reports. After 1960 the AISI stopped publishing estimates of capacity. Nelson estimated the capacities from 1961-67. Nelson's estimates are comparable to the ECE estimates (see Table A.1), but are lower than Bosworth's estimates. Also Bosworth's estimates for 1950-60 differ slightly from the official estimates. Bosworth's data did not become available to us until after the model had been run. To obtain capacity estimates we used the A.D. Little estimate for 1973 which was 163 million net tons/year. Since Nelson's 1967 estimate of 161.8 was so close to the A.D. Little estimate, this implied that capacity remained essentially level during the period 1967-73. Thus we added equal increments of 0.2 million net tons/year. The big change that did occur was a significant decline in open hearth capacity and a large increase in basic oxygen furnace and electric furnace capacities (see Table A.2). The capacities for individual technologies for the period 1968-72 were determined by additions in rated capacity of a technology for a specific location as given by the AISI, Directory of Iron and Steel Works for 1967-72. This enabled us to estimate the operational capacities of each of the technologies for the four regions for 1968-72. The rated capacity is the maximum theoretical output possible. The operational capacity takes into account downtime for maintenance.

Scrap consumption data were obtained from Nelson and AISI Annual Statistical Reports. Scrap prices were obtained from Nelson and BLS, Wholesale Prices and Price Indices, 1965-72. The Indices of Manufacturing Production were obtained from the Statistical Abstract.

Total investment costs for the period 1947-66 were obtained from Nelson. For the period 1967-72 we used the Construction Cost Indices and Nelson's 1966 investment costs to derive the total investment costs. The cash flow payoff periods as defined in Chapter V were obtained from Nelson (p. 380) for the period 1947-66. We assumed the payoff period for 1967-72 was the same as the 1954-66 period.

<u>Payoff Period</u>

1947-53	7 years
1954-72	5 years

The depreciation we used in Chapter V was physical depreciation. In our search of the literature, we found no consensus of conclusive quantitative evidence as to the average useful economic lives of individual fixed equipment. Jack Faucett Associates in Development of Capital Stock Series by Industry Sector, March, 1973 comes to the same conclusion.

<u>IRS Depreciation Guidelines</u>

<u>1947-61</u>

Bessemer	20 years
O.H.	25 years
E.F.	20 years
B.O.F.	20 years

<u>1962-72</u>

All facilities 18 years

The IRS and others argue that fixed assets have been depreciating faster during the post-World War II years than during the pre-war years which accounts for the change in the depreciation guidelines in 1962. Faucett disputes this claim and derive its own depreciation schedule.

Jack Faucett's Depreciation Schedule

1947-72

Special Industrial Machinery 16.3 years

The IRS and Faucett depreciation schedules are quite close for the period 1962-72. Faucett assumes faster depreciation rates than the IRS for the period 1947-61. Based on our conversations with an executive in the can manufacturing industry and Nelson's conversations with executives in the steel industry, it appears that the useful life of equipment will be affected by the time it takes to depreciate it for tax purposes. Thus we decided to use the IRS depreciation as a proxy for our physical depreciation.

Since there are different sizes of open hearth, electric furnace, and basic oxygen furnace technologies, we chose the largest one in each technology as the basis for our investment cost, thus capturing the economies of scale.

The technical coefficients for each of the steel making technologies were fixed for the periods 1947-54, 1955-50, 1961-67, and 1968-72. The first three periods were those chosen by Nelson, from whose data we derived our coefficients. For the period 1968-72 we used Missirian's data. (Missirian, Garo, Energy Utilization in the

Table A.3

Marginal Cost of Capital Steel
($/NT)

Year	O.H.	Bessemer	E.F.	B.O.F.
1947	2.59	1.32	1.47	1.04
1948	2.93	1.49	1.66	1.17
1949	2.96	1.50	1.68	1.19
1950	3.09	1.57	1.75	1.24
1951	3.33	1.69	1.89	1.34
1952	3.45	1.75	1.95	1.38
1953	3.57	1.81	2.02	1.43
1954	5.62	2.97	3.31	2.34
1955	5.81	3.06	3.42	2.42
1956	6.11	3.22	3.59	2.55
1957	6.33	3.34	3.72	2.64
1958	6.46	3.41	3.80	1.98
1959	6.99	3.53	3.93	2.05
1960	6.80	3.59	4.00	2.09
1961	6.85	3.62	4.03	2.10
1962	5.26	3.55	3.96	2.07
1963	5.38	3 63	4.05	2.12
1964	5.53	3.74	4.17	2.18
1965	5.71	3.86	4.31	2.25
1966	5.96	4.03	4.49	2.35
1967	6.30	4.26	4.74	2.48
1968	6.51	4.59	5.12	2.68
1969	7.21	5.09	5.67	2.97
1970	7.78	5.49	6.12	3.20
1971	8.86	6.25	6.96	3.64
1972	9.83	6.94	7.73	4.04

Table A.4

Technology Coefficients

	Units	Open Hearth: Hot Metal Mix	Open Hearth: 50/50 Mix	Open Hearth: Cold Metal Mix	E.F.	B.O.F.	Bessemer
1947-54							
Iron Ore	Tons	1.506	1.053	.512	.056	--	2.180
Scrap	Tons	.349	.565	.819	1.014	--	.120
Labor	Man hr	2.018	1.757	2.017	.688	--	2.255
Electricity	1000 kwh	.040	.035	.027	.550	--	.145
Natural gas	1000 cu.ft.	.270	.330	.700	--	--	--
Fuel Oil	bbl.	.243	.297	.619	--	--	--
Coal	Tons	1.227	.884	.436	.022	--	1.819
1955-60							
Iron Ore	Tons	1.480	1.068		.050	1.58	2.05
Scrap	Tons	.323	.529		1.025	.289	.121
Labor	Man hr	1.845	1.634		.466	1.414	2.117
Electricity	1000 kwh	.040	.035		.550	.033	.145
Natural gas	1000 cu. ft.	.327	.337		--	--	--
Fuel Oil	bbl	.127	.161		--	--	--
Coal	Tons	1.175	.846		.028	1.329	1.521
1961-67							
Iron Ore	Tons	1.478	1.063	Same as 1947-54	.040	1.491	
Scrap	Tons	.356	.577		1.039	.290	
Labor	Man hr.	1.797	1.597		.416	1.661	
Electricity	1000 kwh	.040	.040		.525	.033	
Natural gas	1000 cu.ft.	.191	.266		--	--	
Fuel Oil	bbl	.046	.064		--	--	
Coal	Tons	.955	.687		.031	.976	

Table A.4 (Continued)

Technology Coefficients

Open Hearth

	Units	Hot Metal Mix	50/50 Mix	E.F.	B.O.F.
		1968-72			
Iron Ore	Tons	1.510	1.063	.04	1.40
Scrap	Tons	.310	.526	1.033	.325
Labor	Man hr	1.432	1.36	.80	1.073
Electricity	1000 kwh	.02	.04	.462	.033
Natural gas	1000 cu. ft.	.191	.266	--	--
Fuel Oil	bbl	.046	.064	--	--
Coal	Tons	.772	.587	.03	.772

U.S. Iron and Steel Industry: A Linear Programming Analysis, D. Eng. Dissertation, University of California, Berkeley, 1976). Both Nelson and Missirian develop technical coefficients for each step in the iron ore to the steel finishing process. Whereas we have just looked at the steelmaking process. We have indicated in Chapter VI, the technical coefficients we used had inputs from upstream production (coke batteries and blast furnaces) incorporated into them. We developed coefficients for the four technologies with the O.H. containing three mixes (hot metal, 50/50 mix, and cold metal) see Table A.4.

Prices for the inputs were obtained from Nelson, and BLS Wholesale Prices and Price Indices. The prices of the energy and material inputs include transportation charges. For the period 1947-67 the prices including transportation charges were obtained from Nelson by region. Using the BLS Wholesale Price Indices and Transportation Indices, we obtained comparable prices by region for the period 1968-72. Wage rates for the period 1947-67 were obtained from Nelson, and wage rates for the period 1968-72 were obtained from the BLS Employment and Earnings Statistics for the U.S., 1909-75.

Table A.5

Aluminum Technical Coefficients

	Units	1947-1960
Bauxite	Tons	4.75
Electricity	1000 kwh	18.0
Labor	Man hr	28.0
		1961-67
Bauxite	Tons	4.75
Electricity	1000 kwh	17.0
Labor	Man hr	25.0
		1967-72
Bauxite	Tons	4.75
Electricity	1000 kwh	16.5
Labor	Man hr	20.0

Appendix B

Aluminum

The technical coefficients for primary aluminum production were derived from data in Farin, Philip, Aluminum: Profile of an Industry, McGraw-Hill Inc., New York, 1969. Bauxite prices were obtained from the BLS Wholesale Prices and Price Indices. Electricity prices were obtained from the FPC, Statistics of Publicly Owned Electric Utilities in the U.S. All of the electricity was assumed to have been purchased from the TVA or the Bonnevile Power Administration. This only excludes some aluminum refiners in the Ohio Valley who generate their own electric power.

Appendix C

Can Manufacturing

Data on shipments of beer, soda, vegetable, and fruit metal cans were obtained from U.S. Census, Current Industrial Reports Series 34D. The prices of cans and bottles were obtained from the BLS Wholesale Prices and Price Indices, Capacity figures for neither beer nor vegetable and fruit canners were available.

Until the late 1950's production planning was characterized by minimizing the space required for the storage of cans and one production shift throughout the year with two shifts during the peak season (July-Sept for vegetables and June-Sept for beer and soda). This is based on BLS, Case Study Data on Productivity and Factory Performance: Metal Containers, 1954 and private communications with an executive if a can manufacturing company. A shift was a 40 hour week (5 day weeks and 8 hour days). During a peak season a shift was expanded to six day weeks. Since the late fifties storage has been expanded and two shifts of five day weeks have operated throughout the year. Although can manufacturing has been highly automated since the 1920's, the number of cans produced per minute has steadily increased. Since World War II the number of cans (no. 2 or beer) produced per minute has increased from 240 cans/min. to 1000 cans/min. For the three piece beer and no. 2 cans we assumed the production speed ranged from 300 cans/min. in 1947 to 800 cans/min. in 1970,

Table C.1

Marginal Cost of Capital, Beer Cans
($/Annual Ton Steel Equiv.)

	3-Piece	2-Piece
1963	10.23	4.16
1964	10.49	4.28
1965	10.89	4.43
1966	11.06	4.51
1967	12.75	5.26
1968	13.25	5.46
1969	13.78	5.68
1970	15.20	6.26
1971	15.64	6.44
1972	16.37	6.74

Table C.2

Static Phase Input Data

Beer Cans				#2 Cans 228.65 lbs/ Tons
3-Piece		2-Piece		
Labor Coefficient Man Hrs/Ton Cans	Weight of Cans lbs./1000 Cans	Labor Coefficient Man Hrs/Ton	Weight of Cans lbs./1000 Cans	Labor Coefficient Man Hrs/Tons
	1947-54			
6.01	194.2	--	--	5.10
	1955-60			
4.12	169.7	--	--	3.06
	1961-62			
4.05	144.0	--	--	2.55
	1963-67			
4.14	141.0	12.32	46	2.55
	1967-69			
4.58	127.5	13.49	42	2.55
	1970-72			
3.49	121.9	14.17	40	1.91

and for the two piece aluminum can we assumed the speed ranged from 600 cans/min. in 1963 to 1000 cans/min. in 1970. The speed data were used together with the shift data to estimate annual capacity. Both capacity and production of cans are given in tons of steel or in the case of aluminum cans in tons of steel equivalent. The cost of production of cans for various years by the three piece and two piece method was obtained from a variety sources (BLS, Case Study Data on Productivity and Factory Performance: Metal Containers, 1954, Aerosol Age, Containers and Packaging, Modern Packaging Encyclopedia, Food Engineering, Canner/Packer, Modern Lithography, Tin International, Modern Packaging, Food and Drug Packaging, Brewers Digest, American Brewer, American Soft Drink Journal, Food Technology, Iron Age, Modern Brewery Age; BLS, Monthly Labor Review; Hanlon, Joseph, Handbook of Package Engineering, McGraw-Hill, 1971; Schmidt, Erwin, Aluminum versus Steel in the Can Industry, MBA Thesis, University of Pennsylvania, 1958; Aluminum Development Association, A Symposium on Aluminum in Packaging, London, 1958; Continental Can Company, ABC's of Canning Soft Drinks, New York, 1955; Woodroof and Phillips, Beverages: Carbonated and Non-Carbonated, The Avis Publishing Co., Wesport, Connecticut, 1974, Business Week, November 22, 1976, and communications with an executive of a can manufacturing company). Using the prices of the inputs, the technical coefficients, and depreciation we obtained the cost of producing beer cans with each technology and of producing the no. 2 can.

Investment costs for some years for the two technologies were obtained from the sources listed above. The time series was derived from these costs by using the price index for metal working machinery. The IRS depreciation rates were used as a proxy for physical depreciation. For the period 1947-54 the depreciation was 20 years and for 1955-72 it was 18 years. Jack Faucetts depreciation is 16.9 years. Based on private communications with an executive in the can manufacturing industry, the payback period was taken to be 5 years. The marginal cost of capital is shown in Table C.1.

Since it takes one ton of tinplate or aluminum to produce one ton of beer cans our technological coefficients for the metal inputs will be 1.0 (note: we ignore wastage in this model). Since the two piece produces less wastage than the three piece, this would bias our results in favor of the two piece over the three piece. Since our model shows the two piece to be economically superior than the three piece, our results would tend to understate the superiority of the two-piece over the three piece. After aluminum can output is computed by the model, it is converted to steel equivalent units, i.e. the tons of cans that would be produced if they were made of tinplate.

Appendix D

Model Results

Table D.1

Dynamic Model Results

Year	Iron Ore (1000 tons)		Coal (1000 tons)		Fuel Oil (1000 bbl)		Natural Gas (million cu.ft.)	
	Actual	Estimate	Actual	Estimate	Actual	Estimate	Actual	Estimate
1947	110,153	127,759	97,325	100,527	51,615	33,994	148,936	144,873
1948	113,229	128,728	100,373	101,351	52,275	36,075	167,247	151,501
1949	97,652	106,207	85,381	86,447	43,698	37,532	163,041	151,000
1950	119,820	117,723	97,397	95,851	54,624	37,170	203,852	156,573
1951	130,106	140,915	102,579	114,787	60,088	38,461	208,011	166,312
1952	112,648	121,990	87,829	95,735	53,574	41,850	209,946	172,566
1953	137,433	114,735	101,955	93,750	56,981	48,187	224,864	178,221
1954	104,995	106,763	83,287	86,895	42,817	38,871	280,783	155,462
1955	139,378	125,121	103,674	98,945	54,234	42,214	298,237	284,650
1956	134,029	129,535	100,181	102,334	53,848	41,786	284,813	290,331
1957	139,939	130,662	103,768	103,355	46,791	44,895	282,213	306,633
1958	100,554	91,107	72,233	72,200	38,273	32,895	279,503	221,208
1959	105,725	95,504	77,411	75,780	41,316	35,752	317,876	241,045
1960	114,536	118,666	76,426	83,702	40,452	39,473	361,730	275,707
1961	109,437	100,571	70,840	65,105	36,730	28,530	399,596	354,576
1962	108,080	119,250	68,335	77,232	33,774	29,618	435,237	386,870
1963	116,512	129,967	77,123	84,170	37,497	32,326	465,013	422,427
1964	136,851	148,407	90,336	96,163	39,964	38,065	514,108	489,566
1965	140,394	141,957	92,089	92,108	38,345	37,641	548,793	484,103
1966	143,014	135,032	90,201	87,767	34,546	36,327	518,452	469,495
1967	143,925	142,940	89,576	92,980	29,857	36,876	562,518	485,657
1968	142,583	142,548	88,020	78,835	30,567	29,852	586,850	561,194
1969	143,925	156,808	89,958	86,258	29,476	31,410	634,520	605,136
1970	138,002	188,458	92,278	101,063	29,416	30,312	593,516	624,864
1971	122,015	156,349	79,446	86,479	26,476	30,159	603,473	595,963
1972	134,287	164,239	81,445	90,833	31,258	31,904	636,104	627,541

Table D.1 (Continued)

Dynamic Model Results

Year	Electricity (1000 kwhn)		Total Production Steel (1000 tons)		Capacity O.H. (1000 tons/yr)		Capacity E.F. (1000 tons/yr)	
	Actual	Estimate	Actual	Estimate	Actual	Estimate	Actual	Estimate
1947	21,015	21,525	84,894	85,019	76,174	78,938	3,788	3,280
1948	23,170	23,320	88,755	88,885	83,645	84,205	5,409	6,070
1949	19,701	22,465	77,978	88,349	84,564	86,546	5,931	6,460
1950	24,644	25,464	96,836	92,848	86,759	85,787	6,735	6,450
1951	27,611	26,967	105,200	98,116	91,333	89,559	7,524	6,670
1952	25,945	27,829	93,168	101,675	95,016	96,430	8,253	7,500
1953	31,062	27,705	111,610	101,643	102,724	103,359	8,253	8,630
1954	26,653	26,368	88,312	91,657	109,037	107,635	10,444	9,830
1955	34,838	32,875	117,036	107,442	110,227	109,680	10,821	10,160
1956	35,833	32,857	115,216	107,325	112,315	110,334	10,782	10,560
1957	35,745	34,594	112,715	113,829	116,847	130,166	11,484	12,970
1958	26,476	26,630	85,255	82,914	122,368	117,566	13,267	13,300
1959	27,055	29,077	93,446	90,841	126,542	132,385	13,474	14,990
1960	29,776	32,773	99,282	102,992	126,582	124,654	14,411	15,290
1961	29,740	31,017	98,014	96,827	125,076	119,680	14,857	15,090
1962	31,155	35,194	98,328	104,669	123,504	119,772	15,233	15,360
1963	33,633	36,315	109,261	113,824	122,045	113,174	15,689	15,200
1964	38,865	41,570	127,076	132,294	120,441	113,231	16,112	15,480
1965	40,157	41,855	131,462	132,338	112,893	111,926	17,326	16,070
1966	41,987	42,103	134,101	130,010	105,304	119,873	18,432	18,620
1967	42,511	44,825	127,213	134,411	100,957	107,101	19,577	20,000
1968	46,155	44,833	131,462	136,611	91,492	88,269	20,695	19,688
1969	48,393	47,605	141,262	146,938	79,077	83,126	21,937	19,770
1970	49,582	45,860	131,514	147,348	72,818	80,219	23,253	19,302
1971	48,645	48,609	120,443	145,199	67,858	69,966	24,648	21,092
1972	51,556	50,017	133,241	152,826	60,289	66,395	26,127	21,936

Table D.1 (Continued)

Dynamic Model Results

Year	Capacity B.O.F. (1000 tons/yr) Actual	Capacity B.O.F. (1000 tons/yr) Estimate	Capacity Bessemer (1000 tons/yr) Actual	Capacity Bessemer (1000 tons/yr) Estimate	Bauxide Ore (1000 tons) Actual	Bauxide Ore (1000 tons) Estimate	Electricity (million kwhn) Actual	Electricity (million kwhn) Estimate
1947	--	--	5,226	5,600	2,128	2,284	10,300	10,278
1948	--	--	5,226	5,811	2,279	2,492	11,200	11,214
1949	--	--	5,191	5,182	2,288	2,412	10,900	10,854
1950	--	--	5,537	5,691	2,891	2,876	13,000	12,942
1951	--	--	5,621	5,440	3,695	3,348	15,000	15,066
1952	--	--	5,381	6,351	3,709	3,748	16,600	16,866
1953	--	--	4,637	5,202	4,985	5,008	22,400	22,536
1954	--	--	4,787	5,202	5,845	5,844	26,300	26,298
1955	540	172	4,787	4,273	6,388	6,264	28,200	28,188
1956	540	87	4,787	4,388	7,140	6,716	30,200	30,222
1957	620	1,285	4,505	4,353	6,968	6,592	29,700	29,664
1958	1,479	1,704	4,027	3,730	6,511	6,264	28,200	28,188
1959	2,861	3,009	3,577	3,730	8,027	7,856	35,200	35,172
1960	4,155	4,766	3,396	3,402	8,141	8,056	36,200	36,252
1961	4,650	6,071	3,249	2,899	8,034	7,616	34,300	33,320
1962	7,500	8,161	3,102	2,850	9,878	8,472	38,100	37,065
1963	10,300	9,925	2,955	2,720	10,596	9,252	41,600	40,478
1964	15,960	18,438	2,469	2,490	11,769	10,212	45,900	44,678
1965	23,687	23,310	2,103	2,189	12,622	11,016	49,600	48,195
1966	34,738	35,382	1,737	2,095	13,108	11,872	53,400	51,940
1967	39,906	36,819	1,370	1,963	13,570	13,076	58,800	57,208
1968	49,813	50,942	0	0	13,165	13,020	58,500	55,335
1969	61,236	58,746	0	0	14,574	15,172	68,300	64,481
1970	66,429	70,126	0	0	14,653	15,904	71,500	67,592
1971	70,244	73,293	0	0	14,633	15,700	70,700	66,725
1972	76,584	72,011	0	0	14,359	16,488	74,200	70,074

Table D.1 (Continued)

Dynamic Model Results

Year	Tinplate Used in No. 2 Can (1000 tons)		Tinplate Used in Beer Cans (1000 tons)		Aluminum Used in Beer Cans (1000 Tons)		Three-Piece Beer Can Capacity (1000 tons)	
	Actual	Estimate	Actual	Estimate	Actual	Estimate	Actual	Estimate
1947	2,616	2,600						
1948	2,964	2,949						
1949	2,917	3,192						
1950	3,401	3,159						
1951	3,373	3,498						
1952	3,350	3,478						
1953	3,467	3,463						
1954	3,473	3,545						
1955	3,730	3,548						
1956	3,989	3,728						
1957	3,781	3,910						
1958	3,483	3,764						
1959	3,999	3,808						
1960	3,908	3,917						
1961	4,053	3,853						
1962	3,894	3,955						
1963	3,670	3,844	970.7	797.2	34.4	68.9	970.7	1,056.4
1964	3,709	3,686	1,064.6	889.8	68.9	77.5	1,064.6	1,080.1
1965	3,730	3,714	1,178.6	940.5	77.5	111.9	1,178.6	1,182.5
1966	3,664	3,729	1,406.7	1,021.8	111.8	144.8	1,406.7	1,398.4
1967	3,865	3,682	1,465.9	1,255.6	144.8	170.3	1,465.9	1,573.4
1968	3,774	3,823	1,791.6	1,376.6	170.3	230	1,791.6	1,820.9
1969	3,742	3,794	1,886.8	1,802.3	230	230	1,886.8	1,889.9
1970	3,671	3,773	1,864.0	1,686.8	304.1	304.1	1,864.0	1,864.9
1971	3,705	3,758	1,605.0	1,605.6	383.3	446.8	1,605.0	1,605.6
1972	3,685	3,749	1,489.0	1,360.1	604.1	604.2	1,489.0	1,606.0

Table D.2

Static Model Results

Year	Iron 1000 tons	Coal 1000 tons	Fuel Oil 1000 bbl.	Natural Gas Million cu.ft.	Elec-tricity 1000 kwh	Total Product. Steel 1000 tons	Capacity Utilized O.H. 1000 tons/yr	E.F. 1000 tons/yr	B.O.F. 1000 tons/yr	Bessemer 1000 tons/yr
1947	127,759	100,527	33,994	144,873	21,525	85,019	78,908	3,280	--	2,833
1948	130,323	102,526	35,362	151,048	23,537	89,032	80,606	5,398	--	3,028
1949	95,734	77,915	35,100	139,437	20,889	81,607	75,719	3,708	--	2,180
1950	114,685	92,874	40,492	165,786	26,280	97,874	86,752	6,751	--	3,977
1951	139,882	113,963	41,453	179,267	27,570	106,517	91,331	8,232	--	5,537
1952	101,729	79,812	38,792	155,663	25,540	91,772	81,310	8,232	--	2,230
1953	123,719	101,008	49,792	188,434	29,854	108,167	95,974	10,125	--	2,068
1954	99,412	80,924	36,224	144,340	25,018	85,227	72,660	10,423	--	2,144
1955	131,808	104,209	47,146	318,907	35,496	118,445	109,043	7,256	540	2,146
1956	138,598	109,524	43,507	304,909	34,175	112,349	102,324	7,340	540	2,146
1957	128,053	101,269	44,331	302,038	34,224	112,211	101,715	7,956	540	2,000
1958	92,112	73,023	32,362	217,343	25,001	80,856	73,459	6,657	740	0
1959	101,240	80,334	36,588	249,166	29,888	93,626	81,488	9,637	2,501	0
1960	111,627	78,743	36,901	346,731	30,627	96,017	83,349	9,665	3,004	0
1961	109,345	70,764	27,932	357,351	31,275	96,253	81,573	10,750	3,930	0
1962	118,973	77,026	28,227	370,740	32,064	99,090	80,758	11,059	7,280	0
1963	118,027	76,455	31,641	403,992	35,145	109,978	88,799	11,380	9,799	0
1964	140,900	91,315	37,218	474,113	40,367	128,705	100,935	11,810	15,960	0
1965	145,617	94,467	38,373	494,743	42,517	135,065	98,369	12,890	23,687	0
1966	138,023	89,716	36,513	474,218	43,046	130,997	79,928	16,331	34,738	0
1967	139,328	90,599	34,876	461,471	42,709	127,117	71,789	17,835	37,493	0

Table D.2 (Continued)

Static Model Results

Year	Tinplate Used in Beer Cans 1000 tons	Aluminum Used in Beer Cans 1000 tons
1963	939.5	68.9
1964	1,087.8	77.5
1965	1,194.3	111.9
1966	1,439.0	144.8
1967	1,548.8	170.3

Appendix E

Input-Output Tables

The official 1963 and 1967 Input-Output tables were prepared by the Bureau of Economic Analysis, U.S. Dept. of Commerce. Both of these tables were balanced. For 1967 the work sheet tapes from which the input-output table we developed were also available. Both tables were disaggregated to the 367-sector level and the mining sectors were further dissaggregated by Lawrence Berkeley Laboratory to produce a "400" sector input-output table.

The 1958 Input-Output table, which is domestic based and unbalanced, was produced by the National Planning Association. It is a 400 sector table with the agricultural, metal manufacturing, and construction sectors more highly dissaggregated than the 1963 and 1967 367 sector Input-Output tables. The 1947 400 sector table, which was prepared by the BLS, was unbalanced and was never published. Philip Ritz, Chief, Interindustry Economics Division, Bureau of Economic Analysis made the worksheets for the 1947 table available to me. Also in 1970 the BEA reworked a 90 sector version of the 1947 table. This aggregated table together with the 1947 worksheets were used to obtain the official 1947 coefficients.

We had to subtract imports of primary aluminum from the gross output of the primary aluminum sector for 1947, 1963, 1967. The 1958 table was domestic based and thus didn't contain competitive imports. Also secondary aluminum inputs to primary aluminum had to be subtracted from the gross output of primary aluminum.

All of the official input-output tables have metal cans industry (SIC 3411) as a distinct sector. There are many different sizes of cans. Beer and soda together with fruits and vegetables are the two most common product groups that are canned. Most canned beer and soda comes in the 12 oz. can. Thus the 12 oz. beer can was chosen as the representative can for beer and soda. The most common size for canned vegetables is the no. 2 can. Thus we used the no. 2 can as the representative can for fruits and vegetables. We assumed the metal cans sector consisted of these two segments.

Table E.1

Transactions Estimated
($1000)

Steel	1947	1958	1963	1967	1972
Iron Ore	665,531	909,948	1,133,321	1,592,672	1,874,482
Coal	399,009	411,052	442,571	653,572	1,257,762
Electricity	182,161	210,538	306,066	376,692	487,554
Fuel Oil	75,807	82,566	72,734	77,071	105,921
Natural Gas	43,462	99,133	219,242	249,628	390,331
Steel-Gross Output	7,594,747	14,794,345	20,480,352	23,768,300	37,320,109
Aluminum					
Bauxite	14,892	87,552	129,688	190,527	192,580
Electricity	25,181	72,161	105,243	147,597	213,726
Aluminum Gross Output	171,300	842,508	1,045,476	1,621,424	2,061,000
Cans					
Tinplate	289,414	853,115	881,985	961,211	1,482,994
Aluminum	--	--	44,372	116,826	465,234
Cans-Gross Output	554,340	1,648,976	1,744,669	2,476,748	5,250,239

Table E.2

Transactions Actual
($1000)

Steel	1947	1958	1963	1967
Iron Ore	498,500	862,089	1,168,500	1,496,500
Coal	402,922	474,097	464,000	638,800
Electricity	179,354	190,733	267,000	337,800
Fuel Oil	119,786	122,901	132,900	96,000
Natural Gas	38,296	155,126	222,800	301,200
Steel-Gross Output	7,583,363	14,657,820	19,288,800	23,768,300
Aluminum				
Bauxite	13,875	97,555	130,000	188,000
Electricity	21,910	65,540	114,300	147,400
Aluminum-Gross Output	161,010	800,011	1,069,609	1,682,400
Cans				
Tinplate	316,763	814,676	874,800	1,096,700
Aluminum	--	--	32,900	133,200
Cans-Gross Output	650,872	1,780,206	2,109,700	2,943,100

Bibliography

1. Aerosol Age, November, 1973.

2. Allen and Gossling, editors, Project in I-O Coefficients, Input-Output Publishing Co., London, 1975.

3. The Almanac of the Canning, Freezing, and Preserving, Edward Judge & Sons, Westminster, Md., 1975.

4. Aluminum Development Association, A Symposium in Packaging, Aluminum Development Association, London, 1958.

5. The American Bottler, 1954.

6. The American Brewer, 1963-1964.

7. The American Iron and Steel Institute, Annual Statistical Report, 1947-1973, New York.

8. American Management Association, "Company Studies in Packaging Cost Reduction", Packaging Series No. 54, 1957.

9. The American Soft Drink Journal, February, 1959.

10. Arrow, K., Hoffenberg, M., A Time Series Analysis of Inter-industry Demands, North Holland Publishing Co., Amsterdam, 1959.

11. Arrow, Selma, Comparisons of Input-Output and Alternative Projections, 1929-39, p. 239, The Rand Corporation, Santa Monica, Ca., 1951.

12. Arthur D. Little, Inc., The Role of Packaging in the U.S. Economy, The American Foundation for Management Research, Inc., Washington, 1966.

13. Barker, T.S., "Some Experiments in Projecting Intermediate Demand", Allen and Gossling, Estimating and Projecting Input-Output Coefficients, Input-Output Publishing Co., London, 1975.

14. Barna, T., The Structural Interdependence of the Economy, Wiley & Sons, Inc., New York, 1964.

15. Battelle Memorial Institute, Comparative Economics of Open Hearth and Electric Furnaces for Production of Low Carbon Steel, Bituminous Coal Research, Inc., Pittsburg, Pa., 1963.

16. Battelle Memorial Institute, Technical and Economic Analysis of the Impact of Recent Development in the Steelmaking Practices of the Supplying Industries, Battelle Memorial Institute, Columbus, Ohio, 1964.

17. Battelle Memorial Institute, Final Report on the Potential for Energy Conservation in the Steel Industry, Columbus, Ohio, 1975.

18. Belinfante, A.E.F., Technical Change in the Steam Electric Power Generating Industry, Ph.D. Dissertation, University of California, Berkeley, 1969.

19. Brewers Digest, 1950-1961.

20. Brody and Carter, editors, Input-Output Techniques, North Holland Publishing Co., Amsterdam, 1972.

21. Brubaker, Sterling, Trends in the World Aluminum Industry, Johns Hopkins Press, Baltimore, 1967.

22. Bureau of Census, Census of Manufacturers 1947-1972, Washington.

23. Bureau of Economic Analysis, U.S. Department of Commerce, Input-Output Structure of the U.S. Economy 1967, Washington, 1974.

24. Bureau of Labor Statistics, Handbook of Labor Statistics: 1974, Washington, 1975.

25. Bureau of Labor Statistics, Technological Trends in Major American Industries, Bulletin No. 1474, Washington, 1966.

26. Bureau of Mines, Minerals Yearbook 1950-1972.

27. Business Week, 1976-78.

28. Cameron, Burgess, Input-Output Analysis and Resource Allocation, Cambridge University Press, New York, 1968.

29. Can Manufacturers Institute Annual Report of Steel and Tin Consumed in Metal Cans 1952-1961, Washington.

30. Canner/Packer, March, 1961.

31. Carey, John L., "Productivity in the Metal Can Industry", Monthly Labor Review, July, 1972.

32. Carter, Anne P., Structural Change in the American Economy, Harvard University Press, Cambridge, Mass., 1970.

33. Carter, Anne P., "A Linear Programming System Analyzing Embodied Technological Change", Carter and Brody, editors, Contributions to Input-Output Analysis, North Holland Publishing Co., Amsterdam, 1970.

34. Carter and Brody, editors, Applications of Input-Output Analysis, North Holland Publishing Co., Amsterdam, 1970.

35. Containers and Packaging, 1965-1974.

36. Continental Can Co., ABC's of Canning Soft Drinks, New York, 1955.

37. The Council on Wage and Price Stability, Report to the President on Prices and Costs in the United States Steel Industry, Washington, 1977.

38. Davis, Lofting, and Sathaye, The RAS and LP Methods of Updating Input-Output Coefficients: A Comparison, Unpublished, 1975.

39. Day, R.H., "Recursive Programming Models of Industrial Development and Technological Change", in A.P. Cater and A. Brody, Input-Output Techniques, North Holland, Amsterdam, 1970.

40. Day, R.H., Recursive Programming and Production Response, North Holland, Amsterdam, 1963.

41. Denison, Edward, Accounting for United States Economic Growth 1929-1969, The Brookings Institution, Washington, 1974.

42. Economic Commission for Europe, Competition Between Steel and Aluminum, United Nations, Geneva, 1954.

43. Putnam, Hayes, and Bartlett, Inc., Economics of International Steel Trade: Policy Implications for the United States, Newton, Mass., 1977.

44. Farin, Philip, Aluminum: Profile of An Industry, McGraw Hill, Inc., New York, 1969.

45. Food and Drug Packaging, 1962-1974.

46. Food Engineering, 1957-1973.

47. Food Technology, 1951-1958.

48. Forsell, O., "Explaining Changes in Input-Output Coefficients for Finland", Brody and Carter, Input-Output Techniques, North Holland Publishing Co., Amsterdam, 1972.

49. Fortune, February, 1978.

50. Glass Packaging, April, 1963.

51. Glass Packer, February, 1961.

52. Gold, Bela, Peirce, William, and Rosegger, Gerhard, "Diffusion of Major Technological Innovations in U.S. Iron and Steel Manufacturing, Journal of Industrial Economics, July, 1970.

53. Hanlon, Joseph H., Handbook of Package Engineering, McGraw Hill Book Co., New York, 1971.

54. Hayami, Jujiro and Ruttan, Vernon, "Factor Prices and Technical Change in Agricultural Development: The United States", Sept.-Oct., 1970, 78 (5), pp. 1115-41.

55. Hession, C.H., "The Metal Container Industry", Walter Adams, editor, The Structure of American Industry, MacMillan Co., New York, 1961.

56. Hudson, E. and Jorgensen, D., "U.S. Energy Policy and Economic Growth, 1975-2000", The Bell Journal of Economics and Management Sciences Autumn, 1974.

57. Iron Age, June, 1972.

58. The Japan Iron and Steel Federation, Statistical Yearbook, 1966-1971, Tokyo.

59. Johansen, I., Production Functions, North Holland, Amsterdam, 1972.

60. Jones, Gwendolyn, Packaging, A Guide to Information Sources, Gale Research Co., Detroit, Michigan, 1967.

61. Kawahito, Kiyoshi, The Japanese Steel Industry, Praeger Publishers, New York, 1972.

62. Kawata Publicity, Inc., Japan's Iron and Steel Industry, 1971, Tokyo, 1972.

63. Leontief, Wassily, Input-Output Economics, Oxford University Press,New York, 1966.

64. Leontief, Wassily, Studies in the Structure of the American Economy, Oxford University Press, New York, 1953.

65. McKie, James W., Tin Cans and Tinplate, Harvard University Press, Cambridge, Mass., 1959.

66. Maddala, G.S., Econometrics, McGraw Hill Co., New York, 1977.

67. Mansfield, Edwin, The Economics of Technological Change, Norton & C., Inc., New York, 1968.

68. Mansfield, Edwin, Industrial Research and Technological Innovation, An Econometric Analysis, Norton & Co., Inc., New York, 1968.

69. Mansfield, Edwin, Research and Innovation in the Modern Corporation, Norton & Co., Inc., New York, 1971.

70. Materials Engineering, October, 1968.

71. Metal Containers: Case Study Data on Productivity and Factory Performance, Report No. 71, Bureau of Labor Statistics, 1954.

72. Missirian, Garo, Energy Utilization in the U.S. Iron and Steel Industry: An L.P. Analysis, D. Eng. Dissertation, University of California, Berkeley, 1976.

73. Modern Brewery Age, November, 1974.

74. Modern Lithography, March, 1970.

75. Modern Packaging, 1951-1970.

76. Modern Packaging Encyclopedia, 1954-1974.

77. Moss, Bennet R., "Industry and Sector Price Indexes, Monthly Labor Review, August, 1965.

78. National Provisioner, February, 1959.

79. Nelson, Jon P., An Interregional Recursive Programming Model of the U.S. Iron and Steel Industry: 1947-67, Ph.D. Dissertation, University of Wisconsin, Madison, 1970.

80. Office of Business Economics, U.S. Department of Commerce, The Input-Output Structure of the United States Economy: 1947, Washington, 1970.

81. Office of Business Economics, U S. Department of Commerce, The Input-Output Structure of the U.S. Economy: 1963, Washington, 1969.

82. Ocaki, Iwoa, "Economics of Scale and Input-Output Coefficients" Carter and Brody, Applications of Input-Output Analysis, North Holland Publishing Co., Amsterdam, 1970.

83. Packaging and Shipping, February, 1949.

84. Packaging Digest, February, 1970.

85. Paine, F.A., Fundamentals of Packaging, Blackie and Son Ltd., London, 1962.

86. Paine, F.A., Packaging Materials and Containers, Blackie and Son Ltd., London, 1967.

87. Peck, Merton, Competition in the Aluminum Industry, Harvard University Press, Cambridge, Mass., 1961.

88. Pindyk, Robert and Rubinfeld, Daniel, Econometric Models and Economic Forecasts, McGraw Hill Co., New York, 1976.

89. Reardon, W.A., An Input-Output Analysis of Energy Use Changes from 1947-1958 and 1958-1963, Battelle Memorial Institute, Richland, Washington, 1972.

90. Reinfeld, William, An Economic Analysis of Renent Technological Trends in the United States Steel Industry, Ph.D. Dissertation, Yale University, 1968.

91. Richardson, Harry W., Input-Output and Regional Economics, Wiley and Sons, New York, 1972.

92. Ritz, Philip, Input-Output Structure of the U.S. Economy: 1958, National Planning Association, Washington, 1971.

93. Salter, W.F.G., Productivity and Technical Change, Cambridge University Press, New York, 1966.

94. Schmidt, Erwin J., Aluminum Versus Steel in the Can Industry, M.B.A. Thesis, University of Pennsylvania, Philadelphia, 1958.

95. Schneider, Howard, An Evaluation of Two Alternative Methods for Updating Input-Output Tables, B.A. Thesis, Harvard University, 1965.

96. Searl, Milton, editor, Energy Modelling, Resources for the Future, Inc., Washington, 1973.

97. Smith, Vernon L., Investment and Production, Harvard University Press, Cambridge, Mass., 1961.

98. Soft Drink Industry 1968-69 Annual Manual.

99. Theil, Henri, Principles of Econometrics, Wiley, Inc., New York, 1971.

100. Tilanus, C.B., Input-Output Experiments, The Netherlands 1948-1961, Rotterdam University Press, Rotterdam, 1966.

101. Tin International 1966-1974.

102. Vaccara, Beatrice, "Changes Over Time in Input-Output Coefficients for the United States", Carter and Brody, Applications of Input-Output Analysis, North Holland Publishing Co., Amsterdam, 1970.

103. Vaughan, William J., A Residuals Management Model of the Iron and Steel Industry: A Linear Programming Approach, Ph.D. Dissertation, Georgetown University, Washington, 1975.

104. The Wall Street Journal, 1970-1978.

105. Warren, Kenneth, The American Steel Industry, Clarendon Press, Oxford, 1973.

106. Weinberg, Robert, The Effect of Convenience Packaging on the Malt Beverage Industry 1947-1969, U.S. Brewers Association, Washington, 1971.

107. Woodroof, Jasper and Philips, Frank, Beverages: Carbonated, The Avis Publishing Co., Wesport, Conn., 1974.